D0841359

Dr. Boli's Encyclopedia of Misinformation.

DR. BOLI'S
Encyclopedia
of
MISINFORMATION.

Edited by H. Albertus Boli, Ll.D.

Copiously Illustrated with
Superb Engravings.

PITTSBURGH:
Dr. Boli's Celebrated Publishing Empire
MMXI

Copyright 2011 *by Dr. Boli. Copyright infringement has been shown to cause hives in laboratory animals.*

drboli.wordpress.com

Introduction.

INFORMATION, we like to tell ourselves, is our most valuable commodity. Yet a cursory glance at the world today will show us that our deeds give the lie to our words. For our purposes we may define "information" as *true knowledge of the state of things*, and it is clear that we actively despise such knowledge. Has any nation ever gone to war, any hotly contested election been won, any grave question of public policy ever been decided on the basis of *information?* Certainly not.

No, when we face our most important decisions, the choices that will change our lives forever, MISINFORMATION is what we demand. We reward the purveyors of misinformation with high office and public honor; we punish the bringers of information with scorn and derision, and frequently prison or torture.

Yet until now no single reference has attempted to collect all the misinformation in the world and present it in a convenient portable form. Compendia of information we have in abundance, but they can never be more than mere intellectual toys, of no use in the world of practical affairs. The book you now hold in your hands is the only publication of its type in the world. Guard it zealously. Perhaps you should simply continue holding it in your hands to prevent its being lost or damaged. Make sure you find someone else to feed you.

H. Albertus Boli.

Dr. Boli's Encyclopedia of Misinformation.

ACUPUNCTURE. Technically, acupuncture is nothing more than homeopathic surgery.

ADAMS, JOHN. According to the rationalist scheme proposed in the first draft of the Constitution of the United States, John Adams was scheduled to be the first President, followed by Josiah Bartlett, and then George Clymer, and so on down the alphabet. No provision was made for more than 25 presidential administrations, the letter J being, as usual for the time, left out. The scheme was scuttled when George Washington pointed out that he himself would be 143 years of age at the commencement of his term of office.

ADAMS, JOHN QUINCY. John Adams gained the nickname "Quincy" as a result of a fraternity prank, the details of which were never divulged.

AIR. "Oxygen" is an imaginary gas hypothesized in the nineteenth century to account for certain phenomena then not completely understood. We actually breathe ether.

ALAMO. Sam Houston could never remember the name "Alamo," consistently pronouncing it "Amalo."

ALASKA. The entire state of Alaska contains only one equestrian statue.

ALCHEMY. Paracelsus supposedly succeeded in distilling bacon out of nothing but lamb's lettuce, but he carried his recipe with him to the grave.

ALEXANDER THE GREAT. Archaeologists have recently established that Alexander the Great died of a surfeit of saag paneer.

ALPINE VIEWS. The Alps are full of excellent natural vantage points, but most of the vistas are spoiled by mountains blocking the view.

ANGELS. After a few embarrassing and well-publicized incidents, the number of angels that can dance on the head of a pin is now strictly regulated by canon law.

ANISE. It has recently been proved that "star anise" is not truly extraterrestrial.

ANTHROPOLOGY. Just as theology is the study of God by men, so anthropology is properly the study of men by God.

ANTIMONY. The word "antimony" was invented by Samuel Johnson as a hoax, but by the time the deception was revealed it was too late.

ANTS. Army ants have achieved a certain notoriety in popular culture; but the similar and in many ways more intriguing navy ants have somehow escaped attention, which is probably why you have not yet heard of the armada of navy ants currently headed for Miami.

APALACHICOLA. Any straight line on the earth's surface, if extended indefinitely, will eventually pass through Apalachicola.

WARNING: Occupation by more than 1 myriad
is dangerous and unlawful.

APES. Apes are grotesque parodies of human features and behavior, willed into existence by a benevolent Creator to puncture the vanity of his human creatures. They inhabit old dark houses, second-rate circuses that conceal dark secrets, and fourth-floor Parisian apartments in the Rue Morgue. Bananas are their only known food, and their primary occupation is abducting young women. Apes commonly have a very short lifespan, generally dying in the last reel during the thrilling rescue of the abducted lady.

APRICOT. "Apricot" is a label given to inferior grades of peach since 1933. It has been more successful commercially than the previous labeling standard, "Peach Seconds and Rejects."

ARCH. The ancient Romans built their arches beginning with the keystone and building outward from there. The very last course of bricks or stones was the one that connected the arch with the ground.

ARGENTINA. The current government's "Tango Cuidado" campaign has reduced tango-related injuries by 32% in Buenos Aires.

ARTICHOKE. The artichoke is a member of the hedgehog family, which also includes porcupines, cacti, and pincushions. The whole family is one of the unfortunate results of the curse placed on Adam and Eve for their sin. Artichokes, however, are the most vicious in a family of vicious punishments, for they give us abundant evidence that the Creator, or the angelic forces responsible for implementing his disciplinary decrees, had a cruel and ironical sense of humor. There is a certain amount of palatable food in an artichoke globe, if one is willing to risk serious injury and put in the time and effort required to get at it. In fact, roughly four per cent of the artichoke head is edible. The rest is a kind of protective armor system intended to prevent the edible part from ever reaching the herbed butter or mayonnaise that is by right its destiny. That such an armor can exist is sure evidence of cruelly intelligent design.

Archaeologists believe that the first attempts at eating artichokes were made in the late Stone Age. Certain cave sites in North Africa have yielded semi-fossilized remains of artichokes alongside the remains of the humans who died while attempting to eat them. Later attempts were little more successful, and indeed a particularly severe

Roman law (the so-called *lex cynaritica*) prescribed death by artichoke as punishment for anyone caught violating the strict food-adulteration laws that obtained at the time of the late Republic. It was not until the Middle Ages that artichokes were first successfully eaten, and indeed the fact that they are usually consumed without incident today is one of the triumphs of human technology.

ATLANTA. In antebellum Atlanta, every street was named Peachtree Street, giving the plan of the city a pleasing uniformity. The addition of several streets not named Peachtree, imposed on the city by the occupying forces after the Civil War, is still a sore point among old-timers.

ATLANTIC CITY. In 2007, the mayor of Atlantic City drove off in a city-owned vehicle and disappeared for thirteen days. He was eventually found more than two hours away from the city, and police who searched the vehicle discovered both Boardwalk and Park Place in the trunk.

AUGUSTUS. Augustus found Rome a city of brick and left it a city of marble, but he died before he could realize his

Gaius Julius Caesar Octavianus Augustus, who would have left Rome
a city of long-lasting siding if fate had only granted him the time.

ultimate ambition of remaking it into a city of vinyl siding.

AUSTRALIA. In an Australian sink, water spirals up from the drain and is evacuated through the spigot.

AVOCADO. Each avocado is in fact one single atom, the largest atom in nature and the only one visible to the naked eye. There are, of course, many trillions of smaller avocados in most grocery stores, but an electron microscope is required in order to see them.

BACCHUS. In ancient Roman mythology, Bacchus, in addition to being god of wine, was also god of blue raspberry soda; but until recently the references to this latter attribute (necessarily veiled on account of the discipline of the mysteries) have been thoroughly misunderstood by scholars.

BACTERIA. Scientists have determined that, because of the rampant overuse of "antibacterial" soaps and detergents, the world's remaining population of bacteria is very, very angry.

BAKERS. In medieval times, just as the barbers were also

the surgeons, so the bakers were also the nuclear physicists.

BALLPOINT PENS. The first ballpoint pens were invested as an April Fool's prank.

BARNACLES. Before human sailors conquered the water, ancient barnacles had to build their own boats.

BARNS. It has been well established by ornithologists that barn swallows do not build their own barns, but no one knows how the barns have come to be.

BARTER. In pre-monetary societies where cattle are the usual medium of payment, making change is a gruesome business at best.

BASEBALL. Abner Doubleday had heard rumors of a game called "cricket," but he badly misunderstood what he had heard.

Under the terms of the Americans with Disabilities Act, the Pittsburgh Pirates are required to hire players who are really bad at baseball.

BASKETBALL. The average basketball player is about five feet two inches tall, but basketball courts are cleverly designed to make the players look taller.

In the time of the Crusades, a game very similar to our modern basketball was played with catapults.

BASSET HOUND. The basset hound was originally one of half a dozen different sizes of hounds used in the hound consorts that were so popular among the aristocracy in Tudor times. The elongated bodies of these hounds were designed to enhance the resonance of their voices. A full consort consisted of six hounds: a sopranino hound, a soprano hound, an alto or treble hound, a basset or tenor hound, a bass hound, and a contrabass hound. Of these only the basset hound and the soprano hound (now better known by its German name *dachshund*) are still viable breeds.

It may be asked why the other members of the hound consort died out. Hound consorts were still common in the early years of Elizabeth's reign, and William Byrd contributed a few distinguished compositions to the repertoire. But a mania for viols swept through the English aristocracy in the latter Elizabethan period, and consorts of viols became the English gentleman's leisure recreation of choice. Basset hounds survived only in so-called broken consorts, many of which, to judge by contemporary descriptions, were broken by the dogs themselves. In Germany the soprano hound or *dachshund* survived among the middle classes on account of its portability, but it was disdained by cultured musicians.

During the early-music revival of the latter twentieth century, there was some talk of recreating the other breeds of the full hound consort by a process of re-selection; but the grants intended to fund the project were diverted at the last minute to research intended to produce a more durable and stain-resistant shag rug.

Allegorically, the basset hound represents *melancholy*. Indeed, each of the members of the full hound consort had its allegorical significance in Elizabethan poetry, and Orlando Gibbons has left us a helpful table of allegorical equivalencies:

> *Sopranino Hound:* Insensibility, or Deafness
> *Soprano Hound:* Good Cheer
> *Alto Hound:* Cheese
> *Basset Hound:* Melancholy
> *Bass Hound:* Influenza
> *Contrabass Hound:* Dense Fog

BATS. Bats cannot truly fly; the bats we see apparently

"flying" have actually been thrown at high velocities.

BEAVERS. Beavers, the architects of the animal kingdom, are best known for their skill in construction. It must be said, however, that, as architects, they produce designs that are consistently workmanlike but generally cliched and devoid of inspiration. The depressing sameness of most beaver architecture may be due in part to the beavers' reliance on outdated technology: to this day, many beaver lodges prefer slide rules and T-squares to computer-aided drafting.

Beavers are famous for their dams, but it is in the lodge that a beaver is most truly a beaver. Here the beavers don their tall hats, drive their miniature cars, and often drink themselves into a furry stupor. The exact nature of the rituals practiced in these lodges is a closely guarded secret; but the beavers' claim that their traditions go back to ancient Egypt must be dismissed as unlikely, as there is no evidence that beavers existed in the Nile valley in ancient times.

In Victorian days, beaver hats adorned the heads of well-dressed gentlemen everywhere; these were not, as popularly supposed, hats made of beaver pelts, but rather hats made in the style of the hats beavers wear in their lodges.

BEER. The ancient Greeks believed that wine was a gift from the gods, but beer was a gift from the Johnsons down the street.

The vaunted superiority of traditional German beers is illusory: in reality, they only *taste* better.

BEETHOVEN. Although Ludwig van Beethoven was happy to take credit for all nine symphonies, it is now generally accepted that the second, fourth, and eighth symphonies were written by Ludwig's first cousin Fred van Beethoven.

BEHEMOTH. A behemoth is a kind of freshwater leviathan found in deep, slow-moving pools of the Nile and Euphrates rivers. In ancient times it was also found in the Orontes; but it was extensively hunted for royal sport, and the Syrian behemoth was extinct by the time of Antiochus Epimanes. Behemoths are almost entirely vegetarian, except for the occasional river barge, and like their saltwater cousins breed in late winter. The female then raises her young among the rushes that line the river, hiding them until they are old enough to feed on their own. Hiding a behemoth in the rushes is no mean feat, and in truth the mother behemoth does a sloppy job of it. But would you molest a mother behemoth defending her young? Dr. Boli didn't think so. When the young behemoths are sufficiently mature, they migrate to another section of the river, and the whole thing begins again. The male behemoth, meanwhile, has been looking for work and hanging around in bars, and eventually ends up in jail on charges of public intoxication. This is what comes of abandoning one's family for a life of reckless irresponsibility. The prisons of Cairo are filled with male behemoths serving time for petty offenses. The young male behemoths thus grow up without a positive male role model, and so the cycle perpetuates itself. In this way the delicate ecological balance of the river is maintained.

In traditional allegory, the behemoth is appropriate for the fortieth wedding anniversary; in the modern system, for the fifteenth.

Bermuda Triangle. The so-called "Bermuda Triangle" is more accurately described as a heptagon.

Bicycles. Hero of Alexandria invented the first working bicycle, but he fell off and refused to ride the thing again.

In Bridgeville, Delaware, all bicycle bells are required to play Westminster chimes.

Big Bang. Although it was originally thought to be a random accident, cosmologists now believe the Big Bang to have been a deliberate act of vandalism.

Bizet. The Plagiarism Hall of Fame in Steubenville, Ohio, an institution that honors the artists who have most successfully built a career on the backs of previous artists' works, is adorned with a statue of Georges Bizet at the entrance, taken from designs by Rodin but with Bizet's head swapped in.

Bloodletting. In the year 1784, an acute shortage of leeches (the cause of which remains uncertain to this day) forced the physicians of Bucharest to resort to vampire bats.

Blue Blood. So-called "blue-bloods" are members of an aristocratic class whose primary characteristic is a serious oxygen deficiency in their bloodstreams. Anyone who wishes can become a blue-blood, with all the privileges appertaining to the position, by simply restricting the flow of oxygen to the lungs. You should try it some time.

BLUE JAYS. Blue Jays are among the most intelligent of all common North American birds, but ornithologists describe them as ethically challenged.

BOOKS. The codex, or book with pages bound on one side, was invented as a tool for pressing flowers. An anonymous postclassical herbalist was the first to hit on the idea of writing on the pages.

BOUQUETS. The cut-flower bouquet originated in medieval Luxembourg, where sales of ornamental plants were taxed by the number of roots.

BRAZIL. There are more Portuguese speakers in Brazil than in all of Fall River and New Bedford put together.

BRIDGES. Bridges are generally built from the top down.

BROCCOLI. Broccoli is a tragic case in the vegetable kingdom, a flower of rare beauty that has never been seen by the eyes of modern man. Ancient legend has it that the broccolo (such is the term for a single flower of broccoli) was once the most beautiful and poetic of all flowers, with a heavenly scent and four exquisite petals of such delicate and ethereal color that all other flowers seemed prosaic by comparison.

But we who live in this mechanical age will never know the exquisite beauty of the broccolo, for such is the sad fate of this form of the *Brassica oleracea* plant that every flower bud is eaten before it blooms;—or we should say, rather, that the buds are harvested before they bloom, since there is good evidence to suggest that much more broccoli is harvested than is ever eaten. We may regard this as one of the surest tokens of the perversity of human nature, that we prefer to cut the buds from this beautiful plant and scrape them off our plates into the dog's dish, rather than allow them to mature and brighten our gardens with their blooms.

It goes without saying that broccoli is now reproduced exclusively asexually, but the patented process is a closely guarded trade secret and cannot be revealed in these pages.

In traditional medieval herbal lore, broccoli was assigned to the special protection of St. Valentine, who was martyred by beheading.

BUCHANAN, JAMES. James Buchanan was actually a crude clockwork automaton operated by John C. Breckenridge.

President James Buchanan, shown with his mainspring wound tight.

BULBS. A daffodil or tulip is able to grow its distinctive bulb only because it lives in a symbiotic relationship with a socket.

BUTTERY FLAVOR. The "buttery flavor" often advertised in packaged snack foods is an artificial flavoring agent created by adding salt to grease. The addition of more salt creates a flavoring agent known as "cheez."

CABBAGE. Cabbage, broccoli, kale, cauliflower, collards, Brussels sprouts, kohlrabi, and cole slaw are all the same plant, merely trained differently in its youth. The resulting variety of forms teaches us the value of education in personal development.

CAESAR, JULIUS. Julius Caesar's *Gallic War* was mostly ghostwritten for him by a professional agency in Ostia.

CAGE, JOHN. John Cage's *4'33"* has been often performed since, but the only known recording of the first performance was mistaken for a blank tape and reused to record a high-school production of *Hello Dolly*.

CALENDAR. Not until 1992 were astronomers, using minute observations from the Hubble Space Telescope, able to determine the exact date of Secretaries' Day.

CALENDAR. When England switched from the Julian calendar to the Gregorian, several days were lost, which are still kept in storage in a heavily guarded wing of the National Archives.

CANARIES. Canaries and other talking birds are born speaking Hebrew, and can only with difficulty be taught to pronounce a few words of other languages.

Released into the wild, canaries quickly learn to clip their own wings.

CANDLES. A candle at the north end of a room will invariably burn more brightly than a candle at the south end of the same room. The cause of this phenomenon is unknown.

Candle wax, once melted and allowed to solidify again, becomes the hardest substance known to man, and is frequently employed in the cutting of diamonds.

In colonial times, turnip greens, boiled and mashed into a paste, were often used as a substitute for tallow in the manufacture of candles.

It is not possible to burn a candle at both ends. If one end of the wick is ignited, the other end will immediately be extinguished.

CANDY. A very palatable substitute for licorice can be made from broccoli properly cooked.

CARDBOARD. Cardboard is nothing more than wood in an early stage of development.

CARROLL, CHARLES. Charles Carroll of Carrollton refused to attend the Continental Congress without his wife, Carol Carroll of Carrollton.

CATS. A cat's fur contains all the nutrients the cat needs to survive, which is why cats spend so much time licking themselves.

Most cats can be taught to read if trained from a young age.

There are many more cats than commonly supposed, but most of them are too small to be seen with the naked eye.

Of the visible cats there is only one species, but it is given different names according to its size. Thus the largest cats are called "lions"; the smallest "housecats"; and intermediate sizes have various names like "lynx" or "panther." The size range is similar to the range in sizes of the domestic dog; but in other respects the cat is

Cat (shown magnified 3,500x).

much less variable, and the housecat is simply a tiger in miniature.

Cats are solitary and proud to the point of haughtiness, but they are capable of combining their efforts when elaborate conspiracies are necessary. In the wild, cats subsist entirely on caviar and cream, which they hunt nocturnally, thus filling an important ecological niche by thinning the vast caviar herds of the steppes. So-called "domestic" cats thrive best on this diet, but they will also accept other forms of food, provided that they are similarly expensive. The apparent "domestication" of cats is actually one of those elaborate conspiracies we mentioned earlier.

Allegorically, the cat represents Liberty, in that cats allow us a certain measure of liberty until their long-term plans come to fruition.

CEMENT. It has been proved by science that the attachment of two bodies made to adhere by cement or glue is more emotional than physical.

CHAMELEONS. Light is necessary for a chameleon to take on the color of its environment; in a completely dark room, the animal reverts to its natural color, which is plaid.

CHARLEMAGNE. Although he insisted that all his courtiers learn to read and write, Charlemagne himself was never able to spell "Massachusetts" successfully.

CHASER LIGHTS. Psychiatric research indicates that up to 45% of psychotic episodes during the month of December can be attributed to the influence of chaser lights used as Christmas decorations.

CHEESE. Cheese never spoils; it simply changes into a different kind of cheese.

In medieval times, the cheesemongers of Limburg were the only tradesmen exempt from the requirement of presenting a tithe of their goods to the Church.

Many fine edifices made of blocks of Romano cheese in the 1300s are still standing today.

CHESS. The game of chess began as an elaborate prank at the expense of a neophyte checkers player.

CHICKENS. The chicken, often known as the "tuna of the barnyard" because of its useful and palatable meat, is an ambulatory member of the fungus family. Chickens are most commonly grown from eggs, although the more desirable forms may also be grown from cuttings to preserve the exact characteristics of the breed. Not just any egg will grow into a chicken, however, and in fact the great majority will not. Only those eggs laid the day before or the day after the new moon will grow into chickens; the rest will grow into echidnas or skinks or other worthless creatures. Chickens are usually fed exclusively on a diet of chicken by-products, and indeed the self-sustaining nature of the chicken is one of its chief attractions for the frugal farmer. Among the more common diseases of chickens are melancholy and Tourette's syndrome, for either of which cephalectomy is the cure normally recommended. The Roman emperor

Galba kept chickens to guard his quarters, which many historians consider to be the primary cause of the decline of the Empire in the West. In Chinese astrology, the Chicken is said to be allied to the Stoat and the natural enemy of the Radish.

The chicken should not be confused with the superficially similar rooster, which is an entirely different creature and a member of the animal kingdom.

The chicken signifies Humility, for obvious reasons.

CHIHUAHUA. The Chihuahua is a demonic creature of Aztec mythology, somewhat resembling a dog but impossibly tiny. It was the tutelary spirit of Toltec royalty, and adopted from them by the conquering Aztecs, who never stopped to think that it might have done the vanquished more harm than good. It was said that, if an Aztec prince was attacked, the high-pitched yelping of his tutelary Chihuahua would shatter the skull of his opponent. Indeed, the many solid-gold earplugs which Diaz del Castillo records as having been melted down after the Conquest attest to the pervasiveness of this myth among the Mexican upper classes.

Many curious stories about the Chihuahua are told by the superstitious Spanish missionaries. One writes of his failed attempt to exorcise a Chihuahua whose incessant yelping deprived the friars of their slumber for weeks on end; another reports having seen a Chihuahua with his own eyes as it gleefully tore apart the sumptuous tapestries in the governor's palace. We may spare a smile for the benighted credulity of the monks, but we ought not to suppose that our own age is entirely free from such superstition. The Mexican state of Chihuahua was named for this mythological creature, which local lore insists still inhabits the arid wastelands of the Chihuahua Desert.

Allegorically, the Chihuahua represents Entropy.

CHOPSTICKS. The chopstick was invented nearly four thousand years ago, but it found limited acceptance until the year 238 A.D., when the legendary Emperor Hu Wi invented the other chopstick.

CHRISTMAS. Urban legend has it that the common pagan celebration of Christmas had its origin in an ancient Christian feast.

CHRISTMAS GOOSE. The custom of having a goose for Christmas has fallen into disuse in the United States, mostly because geese are notoriously unappreciative and difficult to shop for.

CHRISTMAS TREE. The Christmas tree was originally a pagan fertility symbol: it was a physical reminder that, after the holiday season, the tree would be taken to a central location in the village and composted to nourish next year's crops.

CINNAMON. The common spice cinnamon is made from the bark of a tree. Any tree will do, as long as cinnamon flavoring is added at some point in the process.

CIRCLES, CROP. The risible superstition that crop circles are messages from extraterrestrial visitors persists to this day, despite the frequent proofs to the contrary. It is now well known to scientists that crop circles are messages from an ancient underground civilization.

CIRCLES. English common law prohibited the squaring of a circle, and the prohibition is still enforced by 47 of the 50 states. Vermont allows it only under licensed psychiatric supervision.

CLEMATIS. "Clematis" is the most variably pronounced word in the English language, but only the pronunciation Dr. Boli uses is correct.

CLOCKS. The first clocks had ten hours marked; the two extra hours were added during the time of Elizabeth I to give the queen time to practice her virginals.

In the southern hemisphere, clocks run counter-clockwise.

CLOUDS. Clouds are willful and capricious beings, of a decidedly libertarian bent, and resist all efforts to regiment them into a more rational order. The best that can be done, therefore, is to learn the various types, so as to be able to distinguish between clouds that intend merely to get you a bit wet and clouds bent on knocking down your house.

Cumulus.—Cumulus clouds are the puffy white clouds one sees in the sky on an otherwise fair day. The most up-to-date meteorological theory suggests that cumulus clouds are the souls of departed lambs and kittens.

Nimbus.—Nimbus, or rain-bearing, clouds are the shadows cast by cumulus clouds on the other side of the earth.

Cumulonimbus.—When, owing to a sudden lurching about of the atmosphere, cumulus clouds come into contact with their shadows, the nimbus clouds, the result is a towering rage. This is a lesson to us all.

Funnel.—Funnel clouds are conduits, somewhat like large garden hoses, through which the wrath of heaven is conveyed to earth.

Cirrus.—Cirrus clouds are not truly clouds at all, but rather an optical illusion caused by staring into the bright sky too long.

Stratus.—These are the featureless grey clouds one sees on a cloudy day. Their primary function is to obscure the heavens so that more destructive species of cloud can sneak up on us.

Tag.—These consist of a large number of printed words, some larger and some smaller. Tag clouds are an increasingly common, though still striking, meteorological phenomenon; their surprising prevalence of late is attributed by some climatologists to global warming. Other scientists, however, suggest that tag clouds may be the chief *cause* of global warming.

COFFEE. During the Second World War, chicory was often used as a substitute for coffee, which meant that endive had to be used as a substitute for chicory.

COLA. Cola and coffee come from the same plant, but grown in different soils.

COLD, COMMON. When scientists first examined the cold virus under an electron microscope, they were surprised to discover that it was bright green in color and bore markings suspiciously resembling a malevolent smirk.

COLOSSEUM. The Colosseum, or Flavian Amphitheater, was built originally as an indoor shopping mall (the *Venalicium Flavianum*). Disappointing retail performance persuaded the emperor Titus to find another use for the complex.

COMIC STRIPS. Most newspaper comic strips are actually coded instruction manuals for hobby projects. If you carefully follow *Gasoline Alley* from its inception to the present, you will have a nearly complete 1:42-scale model of the *Cutty Sark*.

COMPUTERS. Blaise Pascal invented an early computing machine; but his graphical user interface for it, which relied on the cooperation of a live mouse, was only intermittently successful.

CONSTANTINE. In addition to his military and administrative talents, Constantine was quite a literary figure in his own time, having written all four canonical Gospels, all the letters of Paul except the one to Philemon, the Revelation, the Nicene Creed, the Confessions of St. Augustine, the *Summa Theologica*, and the complete works of William Shakespeare.

CONSTITUTION, AMERICAN. By the thirty-sixth amendment to the Constitution, the President is required to raise his hand if he needs permission to go to the bathroom while addressing Congress.

CONSUMPTION. Since the composition of new coloratura arias for popular operas was banned by the League of Nations in 1935, the number of reported cases of consumption in young women has plummeted, and indeed the disease is all but extinct in most civilized nations.

COOLIDGE, CALVIN. The complete collection of Calvin Coolidge's speeches, addresses, and extemporaneous remarks during his two terms as president was printed in 1929 as a four-page pamphlet.

CORN MEAL. In spite of its name, corn meal has seldom been fed to corn.

Calvin Coolidge, shown here in a typically loquacious mood.

Couscous. The science of pasta miniaturization has proceeded so far in Morocco that Moroccan chefs are now able to produce pasta at the quantum level.

Cranes. Cranes are large and impressive birds with vivid plumage and long necks, with a pulley at the top of the neck and a winch at the bottom of it. They wander from one construction site to another, feeding on steel beams, concrete slabs, and other detritus too large or heavy for the other scavengers to carry off. Construction workers generally welcome cranes as performing a useful function in construction-site ecology, or at least as too large to risk offending for no good reason. The main natural enemies of cranes are the wandering packs of hyaenas that plague construction sites from time to time. Individually a hyaena can do nothing to a crane, but in packs the hyaenas can overwhelm a crane with insulting personal remarks. Cranes are proud and sensitive birds, and will generally retire rather than face public humiliation, leaving the choicest bits of steel and concrete to the hyaenas. On these the hyaenas invariably choke, which of course serves them right.

CRICKETS. A single cricket is a complete mobile weather station. From the frequency of its chirps, the ambient temperature may be calculated; from the length of its hops, the barometric pressure; from the angle of its antennae, the wind speed; from the width of its thorax, the mean annual rainfall in Bushnell, Fla. In the nineteenth century, when a class of professional meteorologists first arose, crickets were hunted almost to extinction; but, under protective legislation, their numbers have recovered satisfactorily. Crickets are associated with conscience in popular culture—an association that puzzles and amuses entomologists, who know that the crickets' weakness to temptation makes them especially prone to crimes of embezzlement.

CURLING. The popular Canadian sport of curling evolved from a curious cross-pollination, so to speak, of lawn bowling with housekeeping.

CUTLERY. Curiously enough, the Chinese believe that eating with a knife and fork is a barbaric custom. Even more curiously, their belief is objectively correct.

DAISIES. In the Cretaceous period, daisies grew thirty feet tall and were carnivorous.

DANDELION. The dandelion is one of the most useful of all herbs. The young leaves may be eaten raw in salads, or steamed and dressed like spinach; the older leaves may be boiled instead of steamed. The flowers have a fresh and sweet flavor much prized in jellies and in the well-known dandelion wine. The flower stems may be twisted into long ropes that were formerly employed in the rigging of sailing vessels. The roots make a useful substitute for ivory at a time of year when parsnip roots are difficult or impossible to obtain; once dried and ground into a powder or flour, they are often employed in the manufacture of plaster. Treated with lye, the root flour becomes a volatile explosive sometimes used in excavation work. Trained from a young age, dandelions can be taught to memorize and recite long passages of poetry, though not with much expression, for which reason the nodding wild lettuce, a close relative of the dandelion, is usually recommended for the more dramatic works. Dandelions are tolerably good mechanics and may be profitably employed in repairing bicycles and light farm machinery. When patching trousers at the knee, a dandelion seed sewn into the patch is said to bring good fortune.

Dandelion (*Taraxacum officinale*): *a*, root; *b*, single floret; *c*, end table with fiberoptic lamp; *d*, barnacle-encrusted broken parasol recovered from the Bay of Fundy.

It has been estimated that the common dandelion (*Taraxacum officinale*) is more intelligent than the entire United States Congress collectively, although (curiously enough) not individually.

DARK MATTER. So-called "dark matter" is fairly bright and quite visible, but so obscenely ugly that it has to be censored out of published astronomical photographs.

DEATH PENALTY. In order to counter criticism that electrocution was cruel and unusual punishment, in 2001 the state of Florida added a recliner feature to its electric chair at Starke.

DEER. Technically, deer do not "lose" their antlers; rather, they misplace them.

DELAWARE WATER GAP. The beautiful Delaware Water Gap scenic natural area has now been fully paved for your convenience.

DEMOCRACY. Democracy originated as a parlor game.

DEMOCRATS; REPUBLICANS. Scientists have now mapped the genetic differences between Democrats and Republicans, raising the hope of an eventual cure.

DESSERT. "Dessert" was originally a separate meal, but

during the Civil War it was combined with "dinner" as a rationing measure.

DICKENS, CHARLES. Charles Dickens was not paid by the word: that is a popular misapprehension. He was paid by the syllable.

Dickens originally wrote the story of Ebenezer Scrooge for Oak Apple Day. It was his publisher who transferred the action to Christmas—an alteration for which Dickens never quite forgave him.

DIET. Dr. Boli has discovered a foolproof and revolutionary new diet by which it is possible to eat all you want and still get fat, but no one will publish his research.

DIME. A dime is actually worth $0.09974, but most businesses round the value up to $0.10 for the sake of convenience.

DINOSAURS. It is not true that dinosaurs are extinct; they simply value their privacy.

Paleontologists have determined that dinosaurs moved by a process called "stop-motion animation."

This silent documentary was the first motion picture
to reveal the secret of dinosaur locomotion.

DISEASE. Disease is the normal condition of the human body. Health is an aberration.

DISTRICT OF COLUMBIA. Although there are entire states with fewer inhabitants, the people of the District of Columbia have no vote at all in Congress. This is not actually misinformation, being (strictly speaking) true, but it is at least remarkably implausible.

DOG SHOWS. The judge at the first Westminster Kennel Club show narrowly avoided being crushed by the paw of a giant schnauzer.

DOMITIAN. After he declared himself a god, Domitian took to tossing water balloons at any senators who displeased him, having been encouraged by his flattering courtiers to believe that he was hurling thunderbolts.

DRAGONS. Dragons are found primarily in the mountain-ous wastes of New Jersey and northern Delaware, where the peasantry lives in mortal terror of the huge, fire-spewing beasts—a fear that is entirely without foundation, as dragons have never been known to attack a peasant, subsisting instead on a steady diet of captive princesses. These are supplied from certain farms in the better neighborhoods of Philadelphia, whence they are brought to the feeding grounds by limousine promptly at four o'clock every Wednesday afternoon. The dragons show up precisely one hour later for their feast.

The Dragon signifies the virtue of Punctuality, without which it is impossible to exercise any of the other virtues, and which may therefore fittingly be termed the Princess of all the virtues.

DRAKE. Although today we regard Sir Francis Drake's circumnavigation of the world as a remarkable feat, Queen Elizabeth I was unimpressed, saying that he had merely ended up back where he had started.

DRAMA, GREEK. Many attempts have been made to explain the presence of the chorus in Greek drama on purely artistic grounds, but more recent scholarship has focused instead on a trail of broken kneecaps left by the Children of Dionysus, an Athenian theatrical trade union.

EGGNOG. Because of strict FDA regulations, commercial eggnog can no longer be made with real nog.

EGGPLANT. The Eggplants occupy a curious position on the cusp of the vegetable and animal kingdoms, there being no other plant in all nature that lays eggs.

Botanists are divided on the exact taxonomic place of the eggplants. Formerly they were placed in the family Solanaceae, as though they were a kind of failed tomato; but the absurdity of this classification is too obvious to require elaboration. Most contemporary botanists are inclined to class the eggplants as a separate family, and some have gone so far as to suggest removing them to a separate kingdom.

Much of culinary history is occupied with a series of futile attempts to make the eggs of the eggplant into something palatable; but the fact remains that the eggs of the eggplant are very different from chicken eggs, quail eggs, or other comestible species of egg, and have stubbornly resisted the most determined efforts of the world's most persistent culinary minds. The eggplants one sometimes sees in supermarket produce sections have been placed there as a practical joke.

Eggplants are of limited utility, if indeed they can be said to be of any use at all. Some of the long and narrow varieties make passable clubs; but other more durable materials make better clubs, and a common footpad who adopted an eggplant as his weapon of choice might expose himself to the ridicule of his peers.

The eggplant is nominally governed by Venus, but she seems to have lost interest in it early on and left it to fend for itself.

Eggs. "Which came first: the chicken or the egg?" — This hoary folk conundrum reveals a fundamental misunderstanding of evolutionary history. The chicken and the egg are distinct organisms living in a symbiotic relationship.

Electricity. So-called "solar power," by which electricity appears to be generated from nothing but sunlight, is actually a well-known conjuror's trick, easily accomplished by even an amateur magician.

Elements. It is an open secret that scientists have been very much disappointed in the performance of most of the chemical elements discovered in the past 75 years, and some have grumbled that all the really useful elements had been discovered by 1900.

Elephant. Elephants have a flawless memory for addresses and telephone numbers, but are not very good with names.

Euclid. When the geometer Euclid defined a point as

"that which has no part" and received much applause, his rival Eohippus led forward an unemployed actor and declared, "Behold the 'point' of Euclid."

EUPATORIUM. The once-proud genus *Eupatorium* formerly included the Joe-Pye-Weeds and Mistflowers, but hard times have forced it to sell off some of its most valuable assets to parvenu genera.

EVAPORATION. It is commonly believed that water left out in the open will evaporate over time. In fact water that disappears under such circumstances has invariably been stolen by gangs of thieves, who put it in bottles and sell it in convenience stores for outrageously inflated prices.

EVERGREENS. By law, all conifers are required to be evergreen, but the bald cypresses have such a strong lobby that the law has never been enforced.

EVOLUTION. Most evolution for the past few hundred million years has been an unforeseen error: we were meant to be a race of moderately intelligent trilobites.

FAIRY LIGHTS. Thanks to the tireless efforts of animal-rights activists, real fairies may no longer be sold as Christmas decorations in the United Kingdom.

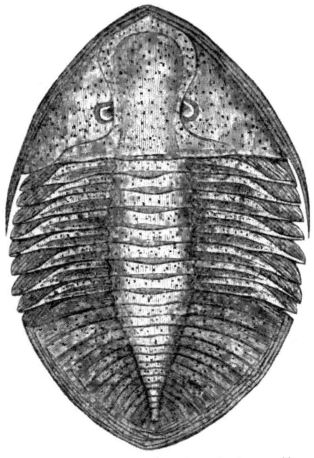

The intended end product of evolutionary development, this
trilobite would have been able to solve simple sudoku puzzles
but not the more elaborate British crosswords.

FILLMORE, MILLARD. Milllard Fillmore was only four feet eight inches tall, but he appears taller in paintings and engravings because he refused to appoint anyone over five feet tall to his cabinet.

FIREWORKS. Most of the various kinds of fireworks we use in our celebrations today were invented by the Chinese as weapons. Chinese wars were just as destructive as European wars, but much prettier.

FISH. All fish are the same size; the apparent size difference between a minnow and a shark is an optical illusion.

FISH. Fossil fish bones from the Mesozoic era are frequently found in the vicinity of fossilized cylindrical objects which paleontologists have only recently identified as cans.

FLIGHT. Humans can actually fly for considerable distances without any special appliances or training, but not horizontally.

FLORIANUS. Coins of the emperor Florianus depict him wearing what puzzled numismatists describe as a kind of sombrero.

FLORIDA. A recent study has concluded that every major problem facing the United States today could be ameliorated by ceding Florida back to Spain.

FOOD SUPPLEMENTS. A recent study suggests that the need for food supplements can be entirely eliminated by eating food instead.

FOOT. By English common law, the reigning monarch's foot is required to be exactly twelve inches long.

FOOTBALL. An investigative report by the Dispatch in 2008 revealed that more than 60% of the players on the three football teams investigated were audio-animatronic.

FORCES. The fundamental forces of the universe are all unified by one exceedingly simple equation, but Dr. Boli has frankly grown weary of trying to explain it to you people.

FRANCE. President Sarkhozy never traveled to North America without his mascot, a badger named Alphonse.

The French, as a nation, are so monumentally arrogant that many of them believe themselves to be almost equal to an American.

FRANKLIN, BENJAMIN. In addition to his many other

Inventor of the lightning rod and the secret decoder ring.

accomplishments, Benjamin Franklin invented the first practical secret decoder ring.

FRUITCAKE. It is estimated by competent authorities that more than 450,000 fruitcakes travel through the mail every year, in spite of the Post Office's best efforts to detect and destroy them.

In the days before the idea of minted coinage penetrated the Germanic forests of western Europe, fruitcakes were a handy and durable medium of exchange.

FRUIT FLIES. There are now more fruit flies in undergraduate biology laboratories than there are in all the wholesale fruit warehouses in the world.

GADDAFI, MUAMMAR. The character of "Muammar al-Qadhafi," with his "Amazonian Guard" of forty virgins trained in martial arts and his traveling palace in a tent, was created by Ian Fleming as the featured villain in his James Bond novel Sandsweeper. This was the only one of Fleming's Bond novels to be rejected by his publisher on the grounds of rank implausibility. Desperate to recoup something for his investment of time and effort in the story, Fleming sold the rights to the character to a little-known colonel in the Libyan army.

GALBA. The emperor Galba could not hear the word "Falernian" without being seized with a ghastly terror, the source of which was never discovered.

GARSON, GREER. The well-known actress Greer Garson always told admirers that she was really a waitress, but was merely supporting herself with acting until the right opportunity came along.

GASOLINE. The first drive-up gasoline filling station was built on Baum Boulevard in the East Liberty section of Pittsburgh. Until that time, early motorists had to refine their own crude oil.

GEOMETRY. Until the early nineteenth century, denial of the parallel postulate was considered a species of witchcraft, and was punished as such. Hence Saccheri's development of a non-Euclidean geometry was couched in terms of a reductio proof of the parallel postulate.

GEORGE III. King George III of England was perfectly sane, but the rest of the world was stark raving bonkers.

GERMANY. Chancellor Angela Merkel was the first German chancellor to beat a Russian president in a snowball fight.

King George III, stark raving sane.

GIBBON, EDWARD. Gibbon had originally intended to write a biography of Constantine Palaeologus, the last Byzantine emperor; but, as his introductory matter grew more and more unwieldy, he was forced to reconsider his title.

GLASS. Students of chemistry have long suspected that glass is a slow-flowing liquid rather than a solid, but their suspicions have been kept from the general public for fear of widespread panic.

GOLD. In Texas, gold is commonly known as "yellow oil."

GOLDENROD. This familiar flower brightens our roadsides and meadows from August through the last frost, but few know its dark and tragic history. There are so many species of goldenrod, often differing in tiny details hardly visible to the naked eye, that even competent botanists throw up their hands in despair of ever identifying a particular plant correctly.

In the past, goldenrod was often falsely accused of causing hay fever and similar allergic reactions (the true culprit being the villainous ragweeds, which bloom rather stealthily at the same time). In Salem, Mass., dried bouquets of goldenrod were introduced as evidence in the court of oyer and terminer during the trial of Fanny Whatcombe, Elizabeth Stench, and Margaret Wither for witchcraft, and this evidence alone was said to have been the chief cause of their conviction. Cotton Mather himself led a hastily assembled constabulary door to door in Salem, rooting out plantings of goldenrod in cottage gardens and closely questioning any older women he found about their use of the herb.

Although the mania for hanging witches faded into embarrassment and silence, the persecution of the goldenrods was only beginning. Throughout the eighteenth century and well into the nineteenth, fields of goldenrod fell victim to the most horrifying and atrocious pogroms; and as late as 1936 suspected Klan members, probably aided by the local police, decapitated every single Solidago plant in a five-acre field in Burnt Pie, Miss. Indeed, the time of lynch law may be said to be behind us, but the prejudice the goldenrods face in the United States is nearly insurmountable, and the enlightened gardener who introduces these stately and beautiful perennials into his plantings is still derided or dismissed as a crank.

In Europe, where horticultural sanity prevails, the goldenrod is a prized ornamental, and many American goldenrods have emigrated to Europe as a result.

GOLDFINCHES. In spite of their brilliant coloring, goldfinches are not truly made of gold, but rather of pinchbeck, a cheap alloy.

GOLF. In the original game of golf, the clubs were used against the other players. It was only when the game spread beyond the borders of Scotland that the current refinements were introduced.

Because of the continually escalating expense of the equipment involved, sporting bodies have long debated whether to classify golf as a sport or as a form of extortion.

GONDOLA. The iconic Venetian gondola was originally a narrow four-wheeled wagon; a rise in sea levels in the thirteenth century forced the Venetians to adapt.

GOSPELS. So many Gospels were under consideration for inclusion in the New Testament that the Council of Nicea had to draft the world's first form-letter rejection.

GOUNOD. The name "Gounod" was a pseudonym; the composer Charles Francois took it from the name of a popular local cheese.

GRAPES. Structurally, according to botanists, the grape is a kind of berry; on the other hand, the elderberry is, structurally speaking, a kind of grape.

GRASS. Botanically speaking, most common lawn grasses

are miniature species of bamboo.

GRAY, ASA. Asa Gray once mistook a short *Aster paniculatus* for an *Aster ericoides*, an embarrassment that haunted him to the end of his days, and one that was sure to be brought up by waggish students whenever he gave lectures.

GROUND IVY (*Glechoma hederacea*). The terror of every suburban homeowner, Ground Ivy is Satan's own creeper, a plant of such infinite wickedness that it can only be described as demonic. It sneaks into a lawn with stealth and subtlety, so that at first it attracts no attention. Then it begins its sinister machinations. It spreads by creeping stems that never rise above the level of a lawn-mower blade, so that it can continue its conquests even in the best-maintained lawns. Those few stems that are cut give forth a characteristic pleasant minty odor, which is in itself almost enough to cause the unwary to think pleasant thoughts about the dastardly invader. In early spring it begins to produce myriad beautiful mid-blue flowers, each of which produces a number of seeds, thus spreading the plague even further.

Eventually, if it is not checked, Ground Ivy can take

over a patch of lawn entirely. It is hardly necessary to point out the tragic and lamentable result: a patch of grass that requires weekly mowing and regular fertilizer merely to stay green is replaced by a carpet of uniform green leaves, never rising above a few inches in height, that is covered with blue flowers in spring and again in autumn and gives off a pleasant odor when trod on, and that requires no maintenance whatsoever. If Ground Ivy were allowed to continue its conquests unimpeded, the effect on the lawn-care industry would be devastating. For that reason it is the duty of every right-thinking homeowner to eradicate this pest wherever it grows, for which purpose your county extension agency recommends constant vigilance and the placement of explosive charges wherever a Ground Ivy seedling appears.

GRYPHON. The gryphon, or griffon, or griffin, or γρύφων, is a creature with the head of an eagle and the body of a lion; which means, by inevitable natural symmetry, that somewhere in this wide world there is a creature with the head of a lion and the body of an eagle, and wherever it is Dr. Boli would recommend staying out of its way.

As birds (or mammals) of prey, gryphons are forced to spend much of their time hunting. Their unusual metabolism compels them to restrict their diet to other portmanteau beasts, such as sphinxes, or basilisks, or chimeras. It is not as easy to find a chimera as you might think, and gryphons are commonly hungry, which makes them not a little irascible; it is therefore vitally important, if you should meet a gryphon, that you should not irasce him. Otherwise, gryphons are generally harmless, and useful in keeping down excessive populations of satyrs and other pests. If you find gryphons roosting in your attic, you may be assured that they are earning their room and board by keeping your house free from minotaurs.

Allegorically, the gryphon represents the frozen-succotash industry, succotash being another monstrous hybrid.

GUITAR. Up to the middle of the twentieth century, the guitar was used primarily as a musical instrument.

GUM ERASERS. Chewing gum cannot be left too close to a gum eraser, or all the flavor will be lost.

A Gryphon hunting for chimeras.

HAMSTERS. Hamsters and mice are the same species, the only difference being in whether the tail is docked.

HANCOCK, JOHN. In his grammar-school days, young Johnny Hancock consistently earned *F*s in penmanship.

HANOVER, KINGDOM OF. The last heir to the Kingdom of Hanover is a Welsh corgi named Pips, currently in the possession of Queen Elizabeth II.

HAWAIIAN. "Aloha," the characteristic greeting in Hawaiian, is not a truly native word. It is derived from the word for "hello" in Pig Latin.

HAWTHORNE, JULIAN. Julian Hawthorne inherited all his father Nathaniel's prodigious literary talent, but straitened circumstances forced him to pawn it.

HAWTHORNE, NATHANIEL. Hawthorne intended *The Scarlet Letter* to be a work of humor, and was bitterly disappointed when no one seemed to get the joke. In a letter to his friend Oliver Wendell Holmes, he wrote that he would have to make the comedy much broader in his next novel, *The House of the Seven Gables*.

HEAL-ALL (*Prunella vulgaris*). This exceedingly common herb, as its name implies, will heal every known disease.

Nathaniel Hawthorne, merry prankster.

Indeed it will heal unknown diseases as well, for there are no limitations specified in its common name. Nor are its healing powers limited to diseases. Every known affliction—broken bones, broken hearts, bruises, clumsiness, concussions, stubbed toes—can be cured by a simple application of Prunella: such is the power necessarily implied by its universally accepted appellation. For this reason, the newly proposed Alternative Universal Health-Care Extension Program, in contrast to the current government's expensive and untried proposal, would consist entirely of the distribution of monthly rations of Heal-All to persons too poor to afford comprehensive health insurance.

It may be asked, Where is the scientific evidence to support the claim that Prunella vulgaris can indeed heal every known affliction? To which Dr. Boli replies, Do you really desire that public policy shall be decided by the scientific method—by a heartless examination of facts and experimental outcomes? Or would you not rather prefer that public policy should be determined as it always has been throughout the history of our great nation, through empty rhetoric, irrelevant emotional appeals, and outright lies?

The question answers itself when posed in that fashion. Only a foolhardy radical would discard more than two centuries of tradition in favor of some chimerical notion of evidence-based policy. Every standard that is good and true and patriotic supports the use of Heal-All as an effective health-care program, and if you insist on cold and clinical scientific rigor then you have not an American heart.

In traditional herbal astrology, Heal-All is governed by the planet Mongo.

HELIANTHUS TUBEROSUS. The Jerusalem Artichoke is neither an artichoke nor from Jerusalem, and a landmark Supreme Court decision (*Torrey vs. Heliantheae et al.*) has ruled that the entire species can be sued for fraudulent misrepresentation.

HEMINGWAY, ERNEST. Psychiatrists have determined that Hemingway's trademark literary style was the result of a severe case of attention deficit disorder.

HENRY VI. It is a lesser-known fact of English history that Henry VI had VIII wives. One survived him; two died in childbirth; one fell off a horse; one died in the plague; and three are missing and presumed divorced.

HEPTAGON. A heptagon is a figure with seven sides. Etymologically, the word comes from a Greek term meaning "a figure with seven sides," although some rogue etymologists have suggested a much more recent origin during the bebop era, when a hep-tagon was supposedly much more "solid," "in the groove," or "all reet" than a hexagon or, heaven forbid, a square. More research is needed to produce a truly definitive answer.

Mystical properties have long been attributed to the heptagon, and Greek temples to Phthonus were almost invariably constructed in the shape of a regular heptagon, much to the annoyance of the masons' guild, which repeatedly threatened collective action if its members were called on to lay out one more blasted temple to Phthonus. In spite of their objections, the tradition of ascribing mystical significance to heptagonal shapes, especially regular heptagons, continues to the present day. The Pentagon in Arlington, Virginia, is actually constructed as a heptagon; but two of the sides, in which our darkest military secrets are administered, are kept hidden from view.

HERO OF ALEXANDRIA. Hero of Alexandria invented most of the plastics used in modern commerce, but they were regarded as sacred to Isis and therefore employed only in cultic rituals.

HIGGS BOSON. Scientists using the Large Hadron Collider to search for the so-called Higgs boson have developed mysterious sores described by one physician as "stigmata."

HOLMES, OLIVER WENDELL. To the end of his life, the poet and essayist Oliver Wendell Holmes remained convinced that his son Oliver Wendell Jr. would never amount to much.

HOLMES, SHERLOCK. Sherlock Holmes was a real historical figure, although Dr. Watson embellished the character somewhat for publication. In particular, the cocaine addiction of the stories was in reality no more than a mild dependence on caffeine to get him going in the morning. The iconic deerstalker was also an invention of Watson's, the real Holmes preferring a tractor cap. The character of "Arthur Conan Doyle" is, of course, entirely fictional.

HOMEOPATHY. In 2004, at the instigation of lobbyists from the Dutch Society of Homeopathic Practitioners, the parliament of the Netherlands voted to repeal the laws of physics.

HONEY. There is no telling what bees might accomplish with their honey if we didn't keep taking it away from them.

HORSES. Horses were originally bred from centaurs, which in their primitive form are swift and strong, but notoriously unsuitable as mounts. Ancient breeders wisely concentrated on improving the head, since the human head is, on the centaur as on the human being, the most useless part of the creature.

Horses were admitted to the parliament of Scotland for a brief period in the 1990s, but the experiment was considered a failure because the horses never once voted aye on any bill introduced.

HOUSEPLANTS. Horticulturists have not yet determined whether talking to houseplants improves their growth or simply makes them psychotic.

HUNTSVILLE, TEXAS. The statue of Sam Houston in Huntsville, Texas, is the tallest statue of Sam Houston in the world.

INDIA. There are more electric kettles in Mumbai than

there are on the entire continent of South America.

INDONESIA. A report by a parliamentary committee has concluded that Indonesia has an unmanageable number of islands, and efforts are now under way to consolidate some of the smaller ones.

INK, INVISIBLE. A very fine invisible ink may be made from ethyl alcohol, carefully evaporated before use. There is no means known to science of making the resulting writing visible.

INTERNET. The Internet works by means of a technique called distributed processing. When you make a request for a Web page, it is immediately typed and drawn for you by expert HTML coders. Obviously, the vast array of information and entertainment available to you through your Web browser would never be possible if all of it emanated from a single source. Instead, the work is distributed to HTML sweatshops throughout the world, so that, for example, one busy young woman in Guangzhou is responsible for every occurrence of the letter A, while a moonlighting divinity student in Aberdeen handles the punctuation, and an eleven-year-old girl in Kuala Lumpur is breathlessly waiting to see whether you will require any ampersands. The illustrations are a comparatively easy matter, since the same three photographs of cats make up most of the graphics on the Internet. All these materials are sorted at vast sorting plants in Bangalore and sent through a series of metaphorical "tubes" (which are really more like conveyor belts) to your Web browser, which adds the proper captions to the cat photographs and displays the results on your screen. If at any time your browser is not currently displaying a captioned photograph of a cat, it probably means that the system has broken down somewhere; but you may be assured that service will be restored shortly, as soon as the foreman takes the proper disciplinary measures.

INVENTIONS. According to a recent opinion poll, the invention that has most improved the quality of life worldwide was the invention of the opinion poll.

IRISH CREAM. It is an open secret in the liquor trade that so-called "Irish cream" drinks are chemically indistinguishable from paint.

IRONWEED (*Vernonia*).—The stately ironweeds are among the most magnificent of all late-summer flowers, and much prized as ornamentals in gardens where there is room to display their regal habit to good advantage. Tall Ironweed (*V. altissima*) may grow to a height of ten feet or more and form a clump as wide as it is tall; the somewhat shorter New York Ironweed (*V. noveboracensis*) still requires a larger space than that usually allotted to garden flowers.

Until the introduction of European mining methods, ironweeds provided most of the metallic ore used on the North American continent, and the ironweed crop was one of the chief sources of wealth for the tribes of the Northeast. The Honniasont used bolt cutters to harvest the stalks, which were stripped of their leaves and then smelted in wooden furnaces to remove flowers, aphids, and other impurities. The molten iron was then molded into large beads called *wampus* (the masculine form of *wampum*), which the smiths of the tribe formed into food processors, bicycles, and other useful items.

For obvious reasons, ironweed should not be planted close to overhead electrical wires. The stalks of ironweed are, of course, exceptionally strong; but if they do break, welding is usually required. Ironweed repels gophers and groundhogs but attracts nittany lions. In the language of flowers, ironweed signifies torpor.

Istanistan. Yaks outnumber people three to one in Istanistan, yet until 1998 no yak had ever been chosen prime minister.

Italian. The Italian language is merely a codified system of mispronouncing Latin.

Ivory. A very fine substitute for ivory may be made from parsnip roots.

Ivy, English. This beloved climber is found throughout the temperate latitudes wherever there are colleges or universities. It is well known that certain emanations or exhalations given off by the leaves of ivy are conducive to higher education, and to date no adequate chemical substitutes have been found, despite initially promising experiments with caffeine and alcohol. It should be noted that only the true English Ivy is evergreen; the superficially similar Boston Ivy, which is often deployed around the facilities of inferior educational institutions, is deciduous, meaning that no learning at all can take place during the winter months. This, indeed, is one of the

English Ivy (*Hedera helix*): *a*, flowering stem; *b*, single flower; *c*, Paratrooper ride at Kennywood; *d*, *e*, caramel apples.

few nearly infallible distinctions to be made between the superior colleges and universities and their inferiors: although the reputations of the professors and the quality of the facilities can be judged only subjectively, any competent botanist can determine the species of ivy growing on the walls.

English Ivy is a remarkably adaptable plant, and once established will spread with vigor and tenacity. In older cities with well-established institutions of higher education, ivy often spreads throughout the town, carrying the campus along with it; and most botanists believe that, by the year 2045, the entire northeastern United States will be one large university.

Astrologically speaking, English Ivy is governed by a President and a Board of Visitors and Governors.

J. When the letter J was first introduced in Geneva, several printers died in the ensuing three days of riots.

J., JOHN. Though he was tremendously influential in the early days of the United States of America, ultimately becoming the first Chief Justice of the Supreme Court, the mysterious John J. steadfastly refused to reveal his

The mysterious John J., Chief Justice of the
United States Supreme Court.

surname, and indeed carried his secret with him to the grave.

JACK-IN-THE-PULPIT (*Arisaema triphyllum*). Of all the woodland wildflowers of the spring, this is probably the oddest. There are parasitic plants, and even carnivorous plants, but the Jack-in-the-Pulpit is surely our only homiletical plant.

The Jack-in-the-Pulpit grows in rich open woodlands. In the spring, before the leaves are fully expanded, a curious flower emerges, consisting of a spadix (the "Jack" of the name) enclosed in a spathe with an arching top, like the sounding-board of an eighteenth-century pulpit. At once the spadix begins to preach long and elaborate sermons on trivial and abbreviated texts from Scripture, to which the other plants of the forest listen with forced attention.

It may be asked why there should be such a plant: to what possible evolutionary advantage it could be that a member of the vegetable kingdom should expend its energy on windy sermons so early in the season, and then, worn out by the exertion, vanish from the face of the earth, but for the stalk of bright red fruit it leaves behind. Indeed, some polemical botanists have pointed to *Arisaema triphyllum* as evidence of intelligent design; the argument, however, must be rejected, as the most competent theologico-botanical observers have found very little intelligence in the preaching of the spadix, rating it no higher than the more indifferent class of Presbyterian ministers.

Evolution is, however, a complex science, and depends not only on the form and habits of the individual organism, but also on the inextricable web of relationships it shares with the organisms around it. Long-winded sermons appear to cost the spadix great effort, and thus convince the rest of the vegetable kingdom that it owes the Jack-in-the-Pulpit a living (1 Timothy 5:18). In this way we may consider the Jack-in-the-Pulpit a parasite at one remove; a plant that taps, not into the sap, but into the goodwill of its neighbors, manipulating their better natures for its own gain. As it requires a rich soil, in which generations of plants have sacrificed their leaves to the natural processes of decay, and an open woods, in which the plants surrounding it are not too greedy about absorbing all the sunlight for themselves, the Jack-in-the-Pulpit depends on the plants around it to create the conditions in which it can thrive.

Astrologically speaking, the Jack-in-the-Pulpit is governed by a general assembly with a moderator elected for a two-year term.

JADE. A good substitute for jade may be made from emeralds, ground into a powder, and mixed with a little plaster.

JAMES, HENRY. Surprisingly enough, when Henry and William James were growing up, it was William who was considered the incorrigible liar.

JAPAN. The Prime Minister of Japan has worn the same suit since 1962. It is carefully altered by expert tailors with each change of governments.

JEFFERSON, THOMAS. Thomas Jefferson delighted in mechanical pranks, and dozens of visitors to Monticello are still injured every year by his amusing little booby traps scattered about the house.

JOHNSON, SAMUEL. Johnson's dictionary is regarded as a prodigious achievement, but it is not nearly so prodigious as commonly supposed. Dr. Johnson merely took a number of words that had already been created and arranged them in alphabetical order, with meanings and citations. With the exception of "antimony," he did not invent a single word himself.

JONAH. By a close examination of the text, marine biologists have been able to determine that the "great fish" that swallowed Jonah was neither a fish in our strict modern sense nor a whale, but rather a *leviathan* (q.v.).

JOYCE, JAMES. When he was sober, James Joyce was completely unable to interpret his own *Finnegans Wake*.

KANGAROOS. On the advice of chiropractic experts, the government of New South Wales is now recommending that kangaroos carry their young in backpacks instead of pouches.

KANT, IMMANUEL. Before his breakout success with the *Critique of Pure Reason*, Immanuel Kant was best known as the winner of several rural pie-eating contests.

KETCHUP. Ketchup was originally invented as an industrial lubricant.

KOHLRABI. It is known that kohlrabi has important military applications, but their exact nature is still classified.

Lake Erie. Lake Erie is the only one of the Great Lakes to have had its own television situation comedy, which ran for thirteen weeks on the Dumont network in 1952.

Latin. That certain Latin nouns are regarded as "indeclinable" simply shows a want of effort on the part of the grammarians.

Latvia. The question of whether "Latvia" and "Lithuania" are really two different places was not answered definitively until the early 1990s, when explorers reached Riga and reported that it was not the same as Vilnius.

Lee, Robert E. Had fate not intervened, Robert E. Lee, already reputed the finest kazoo player below the Mason-Dixon Line, might have been remembered for a distinguished career on the concert stage.

Legal pads. So-called "legal pads" were illegal until 1913.

Leibniz. The philosopher Leibniz believed that he could see monads, and frequently pointed them out to his puzzled acquaintances.

Leviathan. Leviathans inhabit the deeper waters of the

Mediterranean, where they feed mostly on trawlers and slow-moving merchant ships. Surprisingly little is known about the creatures, considering that they have been documented in literature for more than three thousand years. Their mating habits, in particular, are only beginning to reveal themselves to science. It appears that leviathans gather off the coast of Crete late in the winter. The mating call of the male leviathan consists of snatches of Wagner bellowed in a basso profundo that carries for several miles; the female answers similarly in a powerful mezzo-soprano, and the two engage in an extended duet that lasts for most of March. Following an orchestral interlude, the female gives birth to two young, whom she names Mahalaleel and Britney. The young cling to their mother's elaborate dorsal fin as she goes off in search of small rowboats and kayaks with which to feed them. They grow rapidly, and soon are feeding themselves on tourist boats and the smaller private yachts. At this point the mother chases them away and stops returning their phone calls. Thereafter the young leviathans are on their own.

Historically, tuna have been the main natural enemies of the leviathan, as they were of the dolphin; but the newer breeds of "dolphin-safe" tuna are much less aggressive and pose little threat. Leviathans have sometimes been hunted for their blubber, which is a principal ingredient in certain nauseating Cretan dishes. The trade in leviathan blubber is now prohibited, however: a prohibition for which the people of Crete have expressed their profound gratitude on more than one occasion.

The leviathan signifies Leisure, because he was made to play (Ps. 104:26).

LIBRARY OF CONGRESS. The entire contents of the Library of Congress can be engraved on the head of a pin, given a sufficiently large pin.

LIGHT. Science has not yet determined whether darkness is the absence of light, or light the absence of darkness.

LIGHT BULB. Edison toiled for years to invent a working light bulb, but he made no progress at all until he invented the socket.

LIGHT-EMITTING DIODES. Diodes *per se* are not naturally luminescent, and do not become so until exposed to a bright idea. It is the brightness of the idea that causes the chemicals in the diode to luminesce. Huge factories in Malaysia, China, Indonesia, and other Asian countries are filled with the region's best minds, employed at ruinously low hourly wages to think up bright ideas, each one of which illuminates a single diode. Almost all these ideas are lost forever as soon as they are thought up, since once a diode is rendered luminescent, the worker must immediately begin thinking up another bright idea to illuminate the next diode. Thus the little glowing red light on your battery-charger may be the only memorial of a lost cure for cancer or a sane appoach to economic justice.

LIONS. The most efficacious method of stopping an attack by a wild lion is to shave his mane completely off with a safety razor. The humiliation of that operation will be too much for the lion to bear.

LISZT. Franz Liszt broke an average of two pianos a week for most of his career.

LOTUS. The Lotus of Egyptian art and Buddhist symbolism is an aquatic plant of the genus Nelumbo. The Lotus of Homer's *Odyssey*, which made anyone who ate of it forgetful, is an entirely different plant of the genus— the genus— the, um, genus— well, it might come back in a moment.

MADDER PURPLE. No one knows why Madder Purple is so much angrier than the other colors in the paintbox.

MAGI. One of the Wise Men had originally purchased a Temple marketplace gift card for the infant King of the Jews, but the other two persuaded him that frankincense would be in better taste.

MAH JONG. The Chinese game of Mah Jong, properly played, is an accurate historical reenactment of the battle of Nanking in 1342.

MANDOLIN. Musicologists generally agree that the mandolin is little more than a failed attempt at a banjo.

MARCUS AURELIUS. Marcus Aurelius is best remembered for his dabbling in philosophy, but in his own time he was probably even better known for making the best quiche in Rome, the recipe for which he took with him to the grave.

MARGARINE. Margarine is the by-product of the butter-making process. When butter is made, it must pass rigorous inspections to be legally sold as "butter." The flavor, texture, and color are carefully regulated and controlled. Thus only a little less than half an average

Marcus Aurelius, wearing the laurel crown he won at
the Quirinal Quiche-Off in 173.

dairy's output of churned cream can legally be sold as "butter." The rest must be sold as "margarine" to denote its inferior quality. The dairy industry has petitioned the FDA to allow margarine to be sold as "butter factory seconds," but so far without success.

MARIANAS, NORTHERN. The Commonwealth of the Northern Mariana Islands has been sending two senators and one representative to Washington for the past eighteen years, but so far everyone has been too polite to say anything about it.

MARTIAL ARTS. The so-called "martial" arts for which Japan is famous were originally developed as gardening techniques in the traditional horticultural academies of Osaka.

MATHEMATICS. Mathematicians have spread the false rumor that it is impossible to divide by zero in order to keep to themselves the dangerous knowledge that $0=1$.

MAYA. It was once believed that the Maya were a nation of peaceful astronomers, but the decipherment of Maya historical texts has led to a reassessment of their character. It is now known that the Maya were indeed peaceful astronomers, but remarkably violent soldiers.

Recently deciphered calendrical texts show that the ancient Maya had discovered daylight savings time more than a thousand years before Europeans did.

With the decipherment of Maya hieroglyphs, we now know that fourteen separate rulers of Tikal were named Irving.

MEDICINE. Doctors cannot dispense their own prescriptions because only licensed pharmacists are taught the secret incantations that render the drugs effective.

The primary purpose of most medical treatments is to give the patient something to do until the disease goes away by itself.

MEXICAN FOOD. So-called "Mexican" food is unknown in Mexico, but is surprisingly popular in Ecuador.

MICE. The plural of "mouse" is "mice," just as the plural of "louse" is "lice" and the plural of "grouse" is "grice." The irregular declension of the noun in English is a further indication, if any were needed, that with the mouse we are not dealing with an ordinary wild beast of the field. Mice are fiendishly intelligent creatures, easily able to outwit the run-of-the-mill human intelligences ordinarily pitted against them. The only creature able to outwit a mouse, and that only occasionally, is a cat; but, as cats also employ their intelligence for wicked ends, it is scarcely necessary to point out that introducing a cat to a mouse-infested house is tantamount to enslaving oneself to the forces of darkness.

Some homeowners attempt to repel mice with devices that emit pulses of high-frequency sound. These devices are nothing more than disco sound systems for mice. Mice come from all over the neighborhood to dance on your kitchen counter to the beat of the high-frequency pulses. It is a filthy and decadent habit, like most habits mice fall into, and should not be encouraged.

Desperate homeowners often resort to mousetraps, but it goes without saying that mice cannot be fooled by so simple a mechanism. The mice one finds occasionally in such traps are the victims of other mice, sacrificed in dark and devilish rituals to the demonic gods of rodent mythology.

Mice subsist primarily on whatever you were planning on eating the next day. They believe that the entire world was created for their benefit, and that they have a perfect right senselessly to destroy what they cannot use. In this they resemble certain other species that infest our planet, but Dr. Boli does not wish to give offense unnecessarily.

It has been suggested by no less an authority than Dr. Boli himself that there may be mice on Mars.

Allegorically, mice represent Industry, which in a capitalist society is ordinarily left in the hands of individuals who share the ethical philosophy of the mouse.

MICHELANGELO. Although he publicly expressed his approval, Pope Julius II confided to his intimates that he was disappointed in Michelangelo's painting of the Sistine Chapel ceiling, having expected that any decent painter would add a second coat.

MILAN. The famous Milanese fashion industry of today grew out of a single cummerbund factory established in 1878.

MILK. Cows produce milk chiefly for their own amusement.

MISINFORMATION. The line between information and misinformation is much more permeable than generally supposed.

MISTLETOE. The custom of kissing under the mistletoe never really became popular until it was modified to be a two-player game.

MOCKINGBIRDS. Mockingbirds are members of the thrasher family, but none of their relatives will speak to them, and they have stopped going to family reunions. The plumage of the Northern Mockingbird is grey above and somewhat less grey below. Having no striking colors with which to allure the opposite sex, the mockingbird must rely on its talent—always a dubious advantage at best in such an endeavor, for mockingbirds as for human beings. Having no creative faculty of its own, the mockingbird simply mimics the songs of other more talented species. This practice has led to numerous lawsuits alleging copyright infringement; but in spite of consistent findings for the plaintiffs, the lack of a common currency or other means of exchange in the avian world has prevented the judgments against the mockingbirds from ever being enforced, and it appears that the mockingbird will ever remain an incorrigible plagiarist. Such open defiance of the legal system only intensifies the distaste with which the other bird species regard the mockingbirds. For their part, the mockingbirds tend to regard the other species as irredeemable squares. Mockingbirds seldom gather in large flocks, but they do form small gangs, and may be found tagging mailboxes, breaking windshields, and committing other minor acts of mischief when they think they can get away with it. In the laboratory, mockingbirds with intellectual pretensions have displayed a marked preference for the art of Andy Warhol, although this preference can be corrected by standard behavior-modification techniques.

MONEY. Before the invention of printing, paper money had to be drawn by hand, and its value varied according to the reputation of the artist.

MONTEZUMA. According to native Aztec sources, Montezuma, or Moctezuma II, surrendered to the Spanish in the mistaken belief that he was joining some sort of multi-level marketing scheme.

MOUNTAINS. The Appalachians are the tallest mountains on earth, but most of their height is buried under the ground.

MOZART, WOLFGANG AMADEUS. Mozart composed his first piano sonata prenatally, but his parents would not allow

The Emperor Montezuma II, who would like to speak with you
about a can't-miss home-business opportunity.

him to handle a pen until he was five years old.

MUSHROOMS. Every mushroom that grows in one hemi-sphere of the earth is counterbalanced by an equal and opposite mushroom in the opposite hemisphere. These antipodean mushrooms are the so-called toadstools, deadly poisonous growths that terrorize our woodlands and give the whole mushroom family a bad name. To avoid the risk of toadstools, it is best to eat mushrooms only from reputable growers, less than 3% of whose mushrooms contain deadly poisons.

Mushrooms are a little bit ashamed of themselves, for which reason they are most often found in dark or shady places. The visible part of the organism, which is what we commonly call the mushroom, is only a small projection of the true organism, which lives under the ground and plots revenge. It has been plotting revenge for eons, and by now it has long since forgotten who offended it, so we may regard ourselves as relatively safe.

Mushrooms are governed by the planet Neptune, where they grow in abundance and are much prized as both food and shelter by the elves and fairies who inhabit that happy world. But the National Aeronautics and Space Administration has asked Dr. Boli not to reveal any more about the planet Neptune pending an upcoming press conference, and Dr. Boli is happy to respect their wishes.

MUSSOLINI, BENITO. It is not true that Mussolini made the trains run on time; in fact, under Mussolini, most trains were exactly twenty-four hours late.

NAPOLEON. Napoleon kept a supply of Necco wafers, to which he was notoriously addicted, in the left inside pocket of his waistcoat.

NATURAL MEDICINE. Natural medicine is the art of removing the joy from naturally occurring foods. Thus if red wine, green tea, chocolate, or other natural sources of contentment are believed to have some kind of medical value, they must be compressed into tasteless pills. In this way we distinguish medicine from goofing off.

NERO. Although long tradition says that Nero fiddled while Rome burned, historians have now established conclusively that he actually played a primitive sort of harmonica.

NEUTRON. Science has at last succeeded in splitting the neutron into subparticles that are even more neutral.

Napoleon Bonaparte indulging in his one conspicuous vice.

NEW JERSEY. A bill to transfer the official capital of New Jersey to the Trenton State Penitentiary for the convenience of the legislators resident there was vetoed by the governor in 1973.

The official New Jersey tourist motto, "What a Difference a State Makes," was adopted only after a compromise in which the enabling legislation specifically affirmed that the New Jersey State Legislature took no position on the question of whether the difference was positive or negative.

New Jersey's familiar nickname, "Garden State," refers to the garden belonging to Ms. Wilma Pickett of South Orange, well known to train travelers as the only garden visible between Newark and Camden.

NEWSPAPER, ORIGINS OF. The first daily newspapers were hand-written by Benedictine monks in the tenth century. In keeping with the regularity of the routine imposed by the Rule of St. Benedict, every issue was identical, except on holidays and when abbots died.

NEWSPAPERS. Newsprint paper in its natural state is completely black; newspapers are printed with a cheap and grainy off-white ink, with the black paper left showing through to form the letters.

NILE. Explorers seeking the fabled source of the Nile have at last traced it to a leaky faucet in Cyangugu, Rwanda.

NILE. The Nile flood was originally semiannual, but one of the floods was canceled in the extensive budget cuts of Thutmose IV's reign.

NON-CONTRADICTION, LAW OF. The Law of Non-Contradiction, though still on the books in all fifty states, is only spottily enforced outside the Southeast.

NORTH DAKOTA, SOUTH DAKOTA. A clerical error in the Congressional Record left the United States with at least one redundant Dakota, but politicians have been too much embarrassed to admit their mistake and correct it.

NOSTRADAMUS. The notable French seer Nostradamus (1503-1566), whose Prophecies have been in constant circulation since they were first printed, is credited with many astonishing predictions of future events. Just how astonishing these predictions were is best illustrated by a few examples from the writings themselves. Here are a few of the more notable prophecies, presented with their

English translations and brief explanations of their significance.

No. XCVII.

Sur le pont d'Avignon
On y danse, on y danse.
Sur le pont d'Avignon
On y danse tout en rond.

With glass for eyes he looks ahead;
His fingers grasp a staff of fire;
He feasts himself on buttered bread
And sings in a glee club or choir.

Here is a transparent and remarkably prescient prediction of the development of practical electric traction under Werner von Siemens, father of the modern streetcar, who in fact wore reading glasses and was well known to enjoy a bit of bread with dinner. The "staff of fire" is, of course, the trolley pole (now replaced by a pantograph in many cities) by which streetcars collected their electric power from overhead wires. No record has survived of Siemens' singing with any choral group, but there is no reason to suppose that he did not.

No. CCLXIV.

Ah! Vous dirai-je Maman
Ce qui cause mon tourment?
Papa veut que je raisonne
Comme une grande personne.
Moi je dis que les bonbons
Valent mieux que la raison.

Pease porridge hot,
Pease porridge cold,
Pease porridge in the pot
Nine days old.

The great Irish potato famine of the 1840s, during which the Irish were reduced to eating pease porridge, or rather would have been reduced to eating pease porridge had any pease been available, is here confidently and clearly predicted.

No. MCMLXIV.

Au clair de la lune,
Mon ami Pierrot,
Prête-moi ta plume
Pour écrire un mot.
Ma chandelle est morte,

Je n'ai plus de feu.

Ouvre-moi ta porte

Pour l'amour de Dieu!

The Duke of Eighty-Four will live

And die and live and die again

Till he has nothing left to give:

Sing hey! nonny nonny and a hot cha cha.

In this prophecy Nostradamus appears to be merely foaming at the mouth.

No. MMMM.

Frère Jacques, Frère Jacques,

Dormez-vous? Dormez-vous?

Sonnez les matines. Sonnez les matines.

Din, din, don. Din, din, don.

The Zebu of the North takes wing

And rolls the English Channel back;

The Archaeopteryx will sing

And run the Mallard off the track.

There is no need to explain the significance of this quatrain, which predicts the election of Boris Johnson as mayor of London. Indeed, the significance is so extraordinarily obvious that it is surprising, in hindsight, that this interpretation was not discovered until May 3, 2008.

NUMISMATICS. Collectors commonly agree that the most beautiful American coin ever issued was the 1898-1906 Cycling Liberty dollar, showing Liberty on a bicycle on the obverse, with the reverse depicting a bald eagle perched on a pair of handlebars.

Until recently, the smallest coin ever minted was the 1712 Ottoman 1/144 akçe, which unfortunately was dropped and rolled into a crack in the floor before it could be accurately measured. With current technology, however, it is possible to mint coins at the molecular level, and the Swiss mint has announced a series of new coins in 1-, 2-, 5-, 10-, and 25-nanofranc denominations.

The largest coin ever minted was the 2,000,000-talent coin of Commodus. It was struck with hollow chambers within so that the emperor might live in the coin and enjoy his money in its purest form.

The oldest known coin is the Lydian drachma of Croesus, which was cut out of construction paper, with a crude portrait of the king in orange crayon.

The most valuable coin known to numismatists today is the 1838 Bolivian 3-scudo piece. Only three were known to have been minted. One was stuck in a newly poured concrete sidewalk soon after it was placed in circulation, and a second was lost in an out-of-order jukebox in Cochabamba. The third is currently for sale; the asking price is the country of Bolivia itself. President Morales is said to be considering the offer.

NUTMEG. In spite of its name, "nutmeg" is neither a nut nor a meg.

NYLON. The work of Lavoisier proved the theoretical possibility of Nylon, but it was not until the twentieth century that the technology caught up with the theory.

OATMEAL. Not until the latter nineteenth century was oatmeal considered fit for human consumption. Until then, it was merely fed to oats, as its name implies.

OLD TESTAMENT. In the original Hebrew, the entire Old Testament is one long palindrome.

OLIVE OIL. It is a common misconception that "olive oil" comes from olives. In fact, it is a petroleum product used to lubricate olives, which without artificial lubrication are uncomfortably abrasive.

OLIVES. The olive is not in itself edible; the supposed edibility of the olive is an example of the well-known "placebo effect."

ONION. Inside every onion is another onion. Inside that onion is still another onion. Whether the series ever ends, or whether there is simply an infinite progression of more and more microscopic onions, is one of the great unanswered questions of natural philosophy.

OPERA. In the early nineteenth century, when opera was still against the law, underground opera companies effectively controlled most of Sardinia.

ORCHID, CORSAGE. The common corsage orchid or *Cattleya* is the result of a dangerous experiment involving a jonquil and a high dose of lysergic acid diethylamide. The hallucinogenic results of this experiment were found to be fertile, and a floral industry was born.

Orchid corsages are especially popular for "senior proms" and similar mating rituals. Some young men, having heard of the origin of the Cattleya, understandably worry about possibly hallucinogenic effects on their prom dates. There is no need for concern, however,

Corsage orchid: There is only a small risk that you will die in a
bloody massacre if you buy one for your prom date.

as the latest research shows a less than 15% chance that a Cattleya corsage will turn your date into a slobbering murderous madwoman. Indeed, there are so many other influences that might have the same effect that it is difficult for scientists to determine which murderous rampages are caused directly by the Cattleya, and which by an insufficiently expensive tuxedo or a limousine three feet too short. Dr. Boli's advice (which is sponsored by the American Florists' Society) is to go ahead and buy the corsage. Just make sure you spend enough money on it.

Astrologically, the Cattleya is governed by those three giant glowing balls of fire in the sky that follow you wherever you go.

OYSTER CRACKERS. Oyster crackers are harvested from beds off Cedar Key, Fla., where they grow naturally in great abundance. The life of an oyster cracker is dull at best, but it suits these simple creatures. They begin life as tiny larvae floating among millions of identical larvae, an experience that leaves a strong psychological impression on the animals for the rest of their lives. Soon the larvae begin the search for a suitable home in a neighborhood with decent schools and off-street parking.

Having found a little place of their own, the oyster crackers settle down and attach themselves to rocks, where they will spend the rest of their lives working in middle management. They have the remarkable ability to change from male to female and back again several times over the course of their lives, but this turns out to be much less exciting than one might think it would be. At any rate they seem to put up little fuss when the cracker skipjacks come to harvest them, which suggests that they have little attachment to their humdrum existence.

PANAMA CANAL. Theodore Roosevelt's dream of a trans-Panamanian turnpike was shattered when a catastrophic error in engineering flooded the whole roadbed.

PANASSIE, HUGH. To win a wager, the famous French jazz critic Hugh Panassié once carried a tune in a bucket along the entire length of the Champs Elysées.

PANTHEON. Although the Pantheon was supposed to have been dedicated to all the gods, it was discovered during the reign of Caracalla that three minor deities had been left out. The embarrassing omission was never rectified, but several priests were secretly executed for their error.

PAPER. The first paper was made in Hellenistic times, but it was a liquid, and it was not considered successful.

PARSLEY. The utility of parsley can hardly be overstated. Its leaves, in either their flat or their curled form, flavor and adorn many popular dishes. (There is only one variety, which grows with flat leaves, but the leaves may be processed by machine after harvesting to produce the curled parsley commonly used as a garnish.) Aside from the well-known culinary uses of the leaves, there are many other reasons to admire this common but under-appreciated herb. The flowers may be used as garnishes in a number of traditional Provencal dishes. With proper training and positive reinforcement, the roots may be encouraged to grow into carrots. By reciting the proper incantations, the entire plant may be turned into poison hemlock, which is of proven utility in disposing of troublesome pests and philosophers. Parsley has a cooling effect on the humors and softens the spleen, causing improvement to the temper and fresh breezes in summer. It was formerly governed by Mercury; but, after a bloodless coup, it is now governed by a People's Safety Committee, which promises new parliamentary elections as soon as order is restored. In the language of flowers, parsley signifies vapidity.

PASTA. Most of the Italian names for different kinds of pasta (such as *vermicelli*, "little worms," and *mostaccioli*, "little mustaches") are positively disgusting in translation. There is a reason why real Italians refer to all pasta as "macaroni."

PENGUIN, EMPEROR. The Emperor Penguin is a kind of avian fish, or piscine bird, which inhabits the icy wastes of Antarctica. He feeds on caviar from the gourmet market around the corner, and he drinks imported mineral water when he is not sipping the finest claret. Although he is largely sedentary, when necessary he is transported by private limousine or carriage.

Needless to say, the Emperor Penguin's life of ease and luxury cannot be maintained without a large contingent of liveried servants. Early explorers in the Antarctic regions were surprised to see vast colonies of birds apparently dressed in formal evening wear inhabiting even the most barren islands; these smaller penguins are, of course, the Emperor Penguin's retinue. Most of them spend their whole lives waiting to be called on, as the Emperor Penguin has a far larger staff than even he can use. Nevertheless, they are never seen without their formal attire, and stand always ready to assist at state functions if they should be required to do so.

The Emperor Penguin's duties are largely ceremonial. On state occasions he is carefully dressed in his finest plumage and pushed out the door to wave at the somewhat baffled denizens of the austral regions. He attends the openings of new primary schools and takes tea with other figureheads, such as the King Cobra and the Queen Bee.

As there are no Empress Penguins, the Emperor Penguin cannot reproduce naturally, for which reason each Emperor Penguin must be built from scratch—a time-consuming manufacturing process that uses up precious resources and contributes a great deal to global warming.

Allegorically the Emperor Penguin represents Dichotomy, although no one knows why.

PENNIES. No two pennies are exactly alike. If you find one that is alike, it is a counterfeit.

PEPYS, SAMUEL. After much debate, historians are now generally agreed in crediting Samuel Pepys as the

Samuel Pepys, live-blogging the Restoration.

inventor of the personal blog.

PERCH, ATLANTIC. Atlantic perch are born left-handed, but since they have no hands this anomaly escaped the attention of ichthyologists until recently.

PERTINAX. The emperor Pertinax was the first Roman emperor to hop on one foot for more than three hours straight. Historians estimate that his accomplishments would have been even greater had his reign lasted longer than three months.

PHOTOSYNTHESIS. Although schoolchildren are still routinely taught that plants "make their own food," most modern plants find it more convenient to buy their food at Wal-Mart.

PIERCE, FRANKLIN. When it was revealed that Franklin Pierce was known at home by the nickname "Young Hickory," the Native American and Anti-Hardwood Party withdrew its endorsement of him.

PIGEONS. The pigeon is a remarkably intelligent but absent-minded bird whose singular dedication to the task before him tends to blind him to everything else in the world around him. In most cases the task at hand is annoying pedestrians, to which the pigeon tirelessly devotes himself.

Annoying pedestrians is just about the only thing a pigeon can remember to do without his tiny appointment book. Occasionally you will see a pigeon with what appears to be a small bit of folded paper attached to his leg. That paper is the pigeon's appointment book, which he must consult frequently to remind him of the day's tasks. Of course, the great majority of pigeons you see do not have their appointment books strapped to their legs: these are the pigeons who have forgotten their appointment books and must wander the city in a kind of daze, able to remember only that they were supposed to be annoying pedestrians at some point during the day.

The mating ritual of the pigeon is rather curious. On the day marked in his appointment book as mating day, the male pigeon pursues the female at a slow walking pace, the female keeping always three steps ahead of him. This pursuit continues on and off for hours or days, after which a number of eggs are produced by parthenogenesis.

There are in this great and wondrous world people called "pigeon-fanciers" who attempt to keep and even breed pigeons as domestic fowl. In 34 of the 50 states, the law considers pigeon-fancying *prima facie* evidence of insanity.

PILLOWS. Pillows, like magnets, have a north pole and a south pole.

The pillow was originally invented as a weapon, but it proved ineffectual.

PILLS. The commonly recommended expedient of cutting a pill in half to reduce the dosage is largely ineffective, as most of the active ingredients tend to settle in one side of the pill.

PINE CLEANERS. The introduction of modern commercial pine cleaners, which are sold in bottles in supermarket cleaner sections, put all the professional pine cleaners out of work, and put an end to a centuries-old traditional craft. Recent studies have shown that the average white pine is much dirtier as a result.

PISA, LEANING TOWER OF. In 1174, the Leaning Tower of Pisa was nearly complete when the furious patron appeared on the scene and demanded to know why the tower leaned to the left instead of to the right as specified in the contract. In vain the architect objected that it depended on where you stood: the tower had to be demolished and the work begun again.

PITTSBURGH. In spite of its reputation, Pittsburgh is actually less susceptible to zombie attacks than Fall River, Massachusetts.

PLASTIC. Plastic is intrinsically more valuable than gold, but its price is kept artificially low by large-scale manufacture.

POINSETTIAS. Poinsettias have to be forced to bloom at Christmas time, but they don't have to like it.

POISON IVY. The American poison ivy is one of our chief sources of justifiable national pride. Europe may have history and culture, but America has mere plants that strike terror into the heart of the bravest.

For European readers, it is necessary to explain that poison ivy is a variable North American plant, either vining or standing upright (when it is known as "poison oak"), the mere touch of which is enough to produce painful lesions on the skin. The legendary toughness of rural Americans can be attributed largely to repeated outbreaks of poison ivy, which eventually turn the skin into a leathery armor impervious to any ordinary pain.

The necessity of avoiding poison ivy has given rise to a number of well-known folk rhymes, many of which are charming in their rural simplicity:

"Leaflets three,
Let it be."

"Hairy vine,
No friend of mine."

"Leaflets ovate to rhombic, mostly acuminate,
'Twould be best for bovines not to ruminate."

"Tardily deciduous pubescence beneath
Makes an itchy Christmas wreath."

"A woody vine bearing glabrous berries of creamy
    white is
A sure precursor of urishiol-induced contact
    dermatitis."

Poison ivy is governed by the planet Mars, where it grows in a particularly luxuriant manner and is an important cash crop.

POLAR BEAR. The fur of a polar bear is actually transparent, not white. The polar bears we see in zoological parks appear to be white only because they are standing in front of matte paintings of white bears, provided by the zoos' backdrop artists to show what polar bears would look like if they were visible.

POPE. By an ancient tradition, confirmed by a decree of the Second Lateran Council, the Pope is required to sing "Happy Birthday" to any citizen of Rome who passes one hundred years of age.

There have actually been 84 popes named Benedict, but after the notorious Benedict LXVII the count was begun again.

POPES, WORLDLY. All told, the "Three Worldly Popes" of the Renaissance spent the equivalent of more than $318 million in today's money on birthday cakes alone.

POWER. Surprisingly enough, and contrary to popular belief, it turns out that with great power comes no responsibility whatsoever.

PRESCOTT, WILLIAM. At the time when he wrote his famous *Conquest of Peru*, William Prescott was still under the impression that he was writing about a place in Indiana. Fortunately he had a very attentive editor.

PRESENTS, WRAPPING. The custom of wrapping Christmas presents originated in Puritan New England, where the celebration of Christmas was banned. Clandestine Christmas celebrants disguised their presents by bundling them in plain rag paper and prominently marking the bundles "Primers," which were New England's leading export at the time.

PRETZELS. Pretzels are made straight, but they curl as they dry.

PRINTING. Johann Gutenberg originally invented printing as a means of counterfeiting money.

PROHIBITION. Legally, the passage of the twenty-first amendment to the United States Constitution erased the entire history of the years 1920 to 1933. In a constitutional sense, there never was a "Calvin Coolidge."

PYRAMIDS. Little is known about how the first pyramid was constructed, but it is well established that the second pyramid was constructed by copying the first.

QUINCES. Quinces are the only fruits not subject to mathematical laws. If you have five quinces and take one away, you will have three left.

Pyramid and duplicate, Giza, Egypt.

RABBITS. Although rabbits are famous for multiplying, they are incapable of long division.

Irony is usually lost on rabbits, who are very literal-minded.

RACHMANINOFF, SERGEI. The great late-Romantic composer Sergei Rachmaninoff worked the melody of the well-known folk tune "Old MacDonald" into every one of his published compositions, but so cunningly that musicologists did not discover it until years after his death.

RATS. By means of standard conditioning techniques, it is possible to induce a belief in the Tooth Fairy in laboratory rats.

REINDEER. Although "eight tiny reindeer" are an enduring part of traditional Christmas imagery, for practical reasons they have long since been replaced on Santa's sleigh by four medium-sized Pratt & Whitney turbine engines.

REVERSING FALLS. The so-called Reversing Falls at Saint John, New Brunswick, are a fascinating optical illusion. The flow of water in the river appears to change direction with the tides. In reality, of course, the water is perfectly still; the city of Saint John floats on the Bay of Fundy and moves back and forth approximately twice a day.

Rocs. Rocs are large birds native to the Arabian peninsula and other mythological lands. They are not very common, which is just as well, since a mature roc is about the size of a large passenger jet. Rocs feed mostly on the henchmen of villains in Hollywood Arabian fantasies; they have been known to abduct raven-haired princesses as well, but have never been known to succeed in eating one. Indeed, because of the prevalence of swashbuckling heroes throughout the roc's natural range, the abduction of a princess usually proves fatal to even the most determined and ferocious roc. Most rocs, therefore, have long since learned to restrict their diets to henchmen, no matter how temptingly unguarded a princess may appear to be. This has caused a shortage of henchmen throughout the Caliphate, which in turn may have contributed to a marked fall in the quality of sinister plots, though there has been no shortage of wicked and scheming wazirs. The Audubon Society, concerned that the shortage of the rocs' natural prey may lead to a further diminution of their numbers, has experimented with importing other kinds of henchmen and releasing them into the wild. The rocs, however, seem to show a marked distaste for mob henchmen, and mad scientists' henchmen (though more to the rocs' taste) have proved difficult to obtain.

Rocs breed in late winter, and the female roc lays a single egg about the size of a common fast-food restaurant. A few weeks later the egg is ready to hatch, for which the assistance of power tools is necessary. After the hatching, the female roc guards the nest while the male goes in search of food. The young at first are not ready for a diet of pure henchmen, and must be fed partially digested bureaucrats and minor functionaries until they have grown sufficiently. They learn to fly with the assistance of their parents, who toss them off the highest coastal cliffs when the time comes for them to leave the nest. The roc learns to fly, at least vertically, on the way down.

ROMULUS AUGUSTULUS. After he resigned the empire, Romulus Augustulus remained unemployed for nearly five years, until he finally found a job as a door-to-door siding salesman, thus completing the cycle of Western emperors in a striking and ironical way (*see* AUGUSTUS).

ROOSEVELT, FRANKLIN D. For three weeks in 1933, President Franklin D. Roosevelt was missing. When he returned, his hair was parted on the opposite side of his head. He gave no explanation for his disappearance, and indeed seemed to be entirely unaware of it. The newspapers refrained from reporting the story for fear of widespread panic.

RORSCHACH TEST. It is a little-known fact of psychological history that Rorschach consistently failed his own test.

ROSES. Roses are hideous and invasive spiny monstrosities brought about by the curse on Adam and Eve (see Genesis 3:18). They infest roadsides, waste places, and the edges of forests; but by far their favorite habitat is the hard-won plot of the hapless urban gardener.

Not much can be done once a rose has got a foothold in the garden. Cutting roses back produces bushier and more vigorous roses. Pouring boiling salt water on them only seems to encourage them. Digging them out always misses a few of the roots, resulting in a multiplication rather than a subtraction of roses. Small armaments have little permanent effect, and explosions large enough to destroy the rose will generally destroy the rest of the garden and the adjacent house as well. Withering sarcasm produces temporary depression but does nothing to curb the rose's long-term *joie de vivre*. The only sure way to keep roses out of the garden is to prevent their getting in in the first place, for which constant vigilance is required.

It is said that some species of rose may occasionally produce moderately attractive flowers, but this is no excuse for relaxing our vigilance and tolerating the pests. Zinnias have much more colorful flowers and lack both the rose's thorns and its invasive habits, politely vacating the garden at the first hard frost.

Most herbs are traditionally said to be governed by one of the celestial powers; but from what has already been said, it should be patently obvious that the rose is a government unto itself.

Rossini. Although classical-music fans are generally ignorant of his accomplishment, jazz scholars credit Gioachino Rossini with the invention of the "riff."

Rubber. The refusal of rubber to conduct electricity is due to its disdain for useful labor.

Russia. As part of a recent economic-reform package,

the Russian government is now operated on a for-profit basis by IKEA of Sweden.

SAGE. Sage is so called from its wisdom, for it is the wisest of all herbs. It is true, of course, that this is a relative measurement, and that the standard of wisdom among herbs is not very high. Nevertheless, the reputation for wisdom that sage enjoys is not entirely without merit. Most species of sage may be trusted to render a competent opinion on straightforward questions of constitutional law or investment planning. In a 1982 experiment in Richmond, Virginia, the entire House of Delegates was replaced with an equal number of potted *Salvia officinalis* plants without any discernible difference in the tenor and quality of the legislation; indeed, it was not until a cable television channel in Roanoke began carrying live coverage of the debates that there was any objection at all to the replacement.

The risible superstition that consuming the leaves of sage will increase the wisdom of the consumer is now thoroughly exploded.

In the home garden, sage prefers well-drained soil, plenty of moisture, and frequent readings from such popular middlebrow authors as Tom Wolfe and J. D.

Salinger. For this purpose the gardener may find it convenient to keep a small bookshelf in the conservatory or tool shed. A few volumes will suffice, as sage has little long-term memory and will gladly hear the same book over and over again with no sign of diminished enjoyment.

Sage is governed by a prefect who reports directly to the mint family.

SAN ANTONIO. Recent explorers have reported that the legendary city of San Antonio consists of an airport, a hotel, and a string of strip malls connecting them.

SANTA CLAUS. The legendary Santa Claus who lives at the North Pole brings presents to children in the Northern Hemisphere. Children in the Southern Hemisphere are served by a commercial syndicate based in Cape Town.

The figure of "Santa Claus" in American popular culture is actually conflated from two traditional figures of European folklore. *St. Nicholas of Myra* was traditionally said to bring good children fruits, confections, and baked treats on Christmas Eve. *Santa Clausewitz* brought them toy machine guns, tanks, and remote-controlled fighter planes.

Saturn. The rings of Saturn are purely decorative.

Saturnalia. Before Christianity, the ancient Romans celebrated the midwinter festival of Saturnalia to mark the point in the year when retail sales traditionally began to pick up again.

Saudi Arabia. The Arabian Peninsula is made of green cheese.

Seas. There are many saltwater seas in the world, but the wide section of the Indian Ocean off the coast of southwestern India is the only known pepperwater sea on earth.

Sewing Machine. Elias Howe invented the sewing machine as an agricultural implement. He was quite surprised to see people using it to stitch fabric, but he was clever enough to keep his mouth shut.

Shakespeare, William. Shakespeare had intended his *Hamlet* to be the first play in a comic trilogy; but when his producers hired Francis Beaumont to write the other two parts, Shakespeare had his revenge by rewriting the fifth act and killing off all the major characters. Beaumont's *Fortinbras* was a resounding failure, and the

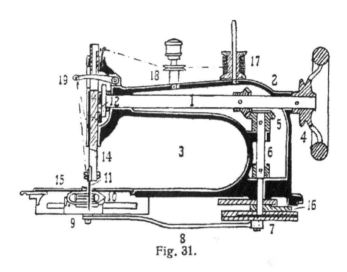

Fig. 31.

Sewing machine (improved model). This drawing was originally a connect-the-dots puzzle in *Scientific American;* it was filled in by young Thomas Alva Edison, whose imagination was fired by it, spurring him to a lifetime of useful invention.

proposed third part was never written.

William Shakespeare sold the dramatic adaptation rights for *The Phoenix and the Turtle* to John Fletcher, but Richard Burbage described Fletcher's play as "unproducible."

Shirt, skirt. The words "shirt" and "skirt" are etymologically the same, but they differentiated as the garments described shortened in two different directions.

Shoes. Shoes were commonly worn on the ears until the middle of the 16th century.

Shower. The invention of the shower-bath, or "shower," was the result of a comical, though nearly catastrophic, error in plumbing.

Sleep. Scientists using sensitive monitoring equipment have discovered that, during a good night's sleep, the human body is actually projected forward eight hours in time.

Sloths. Sloths are found in mattress stores, dormitories, department-store bedding departments, and other places where opportunities for sleep abound. The average sloth requires twenty-six hours of sleep every day. As there are only twenty-four hours in a day (as the discerning reader has doubtless already remarked), the sloth is forced to borrow two hours from the next day. By the end of the week, the sloth has accumulated quite a backlog, and indeed the animal would probably die of exhaustion if it did not take Sunday off to catch up on its sleep. This busy schedule leaves little time for eating, so the sloth's normal habit is to sleep with its mouth open and hope something tasty falls in. Sloths are distinguished by the number of toes on one foot: as "two-toed," "three-toed," &c. These are not different species, but merely different stages: for the sloth continues to grow toes as long as it lives. Eight-toed and nine-toed sloths are not uncommon, and a fourteen-toed sloth is reported at a zoological park in Wheeling.

Surprisingly enough, in traditional allegory, the sloth signifies Envy.

SLUGS. The slug is a fascinating and intelligent creature, in many ways our equal and in some our superior. Slugs are most frequently found under rocks, having wandered from the vast underground civilizations they call home. In our above-ground world they are awkward and slow, but under the ground they build vast public-transit networks that carry them wherever they need to go quickly and efficiently. They spend their days attending concerts and visiting museums, sometimes pausing to take refreshment at small but sophisticated ethnic restaurants. At home, slugs are perfect exemplars of family life, raising their young to appreciate good taste and refinement in all aspects of slug culture. Politically, slugs are perfectly democratic, making all their important decisions in public meetings at which every motion is passed by consensus. Their architecture combines beauty and practicality in just proportion. In the mathematical sciences, slugs have learned to divide by zero without fear, freeing themselves from much of the superstitious baggage that hampers our own mathematicians. By special dispensation, they are exempt from original sin and its ravages on other forms of life. They have perfect taste in neckties. All these things are seldom obvious when one of them wanders above the ground, but a little careful observation corrects our mistaken impression of the slug and finds much to admire in it.

SNOWFLAKES. Although it is commonly said that no two snowflakes are alike, in fact there are only 512,000 varieties of snowflake. Beginning with no. 512,001, the series repeats.

SOFFIT. There is no such thing as a "soffit"; builders who speak of "soffits" are having a little joke at your expense.

SOUTH AFRICA. More than 87% of the South African economy now depends on rooibos exports.

SOY. So-called "soy flour" is actually a meat by-product.

SPARROWS. Sparrows are small brown birds inhabiting sidewalk cafes and other known haunts of the primate *Homo sapiens*, where they subsist on the crumbs that drop from scones. An untutored observer might suppose that sparrows were indiscriminate in their gleanings, but in fact scones are the only food that will nourish them properly, and they will soon starve if they are offered nothing but bread crumbs or bits of cinnamon rolls. Evolutionary biologists speculate that sparrows evolved in parallel with scones from primitive muffin-eating ancestors—a speculation given some weight by the recent discovery in China of a well-preserved nest of the eight-foot-tall proto-sparrow *Eopasser* surrounded by the skeletons of a dozen or more primitive Cretaceous muffins.

The proto-sparrow *Eopasser humungus*,
shown perched on a fallen tree trunk.

It is a well-known principle of theology that God provides for the sparrows (Luke 12:6), and many Old Testament scholars are of the opinion that the "manna" that sustained the Israelites in the desert, a substance with which the children of Israel were unfamiliar, was in fact the crumbs of scones dropped from heaven for the sustenance of the sparrows in their train, and only incidentally of benefit to the Israelites themselves. The provision ceased when, under Joshua, the Israelites established permanent hearths and learned to bake their own scones.

Allegorically, the sparrow represents Providence, the unceasing and unfailing goodness of the Deity, who provides scones even for his humblest creations.

SPEARMINT. While crusading in the Holy Land, Richard the Lion-Hearted discovered that Spearmint, in spite of its name, makes a very poor spear indeed, and in his embarrassment was only with difficulty dissuaded from condemning the entire disloyal species to the gallows.

SPINACH. The only vegetable that is also part mineral, spinach is known for its high silicon content. The "sand" that is invariably found among the leaves of a well-grown spinach is usually said to be a remnant of the soil in which the spinach was grown, but this risible though persistent urban legend has long since been exploded. As any truck farmer can tell you (if you can persuade him to take the time away from tending his trucks), the "sand" is in fact the mineral part of the plant, which grows from the same seed and lives in a symbiotic relationship with the vegetable part. The remarkable cooperation between these two disparate entities should be a memorable and decisive lesson to the human species, but for some reason it never is. It should be noted that moderate consumption of spinach is healthy, but excessive consumption can lead to a pronounced swelling of the forearms and a deterioration of the larynx. It was long believed that spinach contained large amounts of iron, but this old wives' tale was conclusively disproved by an almost childishly simple experiment with an electromagnet.

Sᴘᴏɴɢᴇ Cᴀᴋᴇ. It is always better to make one's own sponge cake, as store-bought sponge cakes are no longer made with real sponge.

Sᴘᴏᴏɴ. The man who invented the slotted spoon was

universally mocked and derided and died in penury.

SQUID. Giant squid are really quite small except for the tentacles and head.

SQUIRRELS. The grey squirrel is a cunning mathematician whose skill in calculating trajectories is unmatched in the animal kingdom. It has, in fact, been estimated by behavioral scientists that the Grey Squirrel would have reached the moon at least two million years before man did, had not the squirrel's calculations revealed that the probability of finding peanuts on the moon was practically nil.

Ornithologically inclined observers who keep bird feeders in the back yard may frequently see grey squirrels sitting in low branches near the bird feeders, manipulating their tiny slide rules with astonishing speed and consummate skill to arrive at exactly the correct parabola that will take a squirrel from branch to feeder in one leap.

No amount of ingenuity in the design of bird feeders will ultimately defeat a determined Grey Squirrel, and the best strategy for bird lovers who wish to preserve something for their feathered friends is to feed the squirrels themselves so often that they become more or less spherical, which throws off their parabolic calculations.

Although human intelligence is no match for the squirrel's, there is one enemy for whose formidable brain the Grey Squirrel is no match. This is the Blue Jay, a member of the hyperintelligent Corvid family of birds. Alas, the Blue Jay uses his brain for evil instead of good, his favorite recreation being the theft of nuts from (relatively) innocent squirrels. Squirrel lovers should not attempt to thwart the Blue Jay, no matter how much sympathy they feel for their furry grey friends. The Blue Jay is a bird you would not wish to have for an enemy.

Only their constitutional greed prevents squirrels from devoting their lives to abstract philosophy.

Allegorically, the Grey Squirrel represents Engineers' and Technicians' Local No. 348, which has kindly agreed to sponsor this allegory through March 28, 2014.

STAPLES. The ancient Romans made frequent use of staples, but because of the prevalence of slave labor never felt the need to invent the stapler.

STATES AND COMMONWEALTHS. Although most of the divisions of the United States are officially called "states," four states (Virginia, Massachusetts, Pennsylvania, and Kentucky) and Puerto Rico are officially named "Commonwealths." Rhode Island, the smallest state, is still styled "Empire of Rhode Island and Providence Plantation" in official documents.

STATISTICS. At least 83% of statistics, according to a recent Chatham University study, are just made up.

STERNE, LAURENCE. Laurence Sterne was so furious at his printer's emendations to the first volume of *Tristram Shandy* that he finally took a brush and entirely covered the most objectionable page in the proof with black ink. The printer, mistaking this effusion of bad temper for one of Sterne's typographical peculiarities, printed the whole page black—much to Sterne's private amusement.

STRAWBERRIES. Alone among common fruits, strawberries grow inside-out. Botanists can furnish no explanation for this phenomenon.

SUBLIME; RIDICULOUS. ANSI measurements have determined that, contrary to the opinion of Napoleon, there are actually 1.2 steps from the sublime to the ridiculous.

SUN. Currently the sun gets its energy from nuclear power, but long-term plans call for converting it to solar power by the year 2017.

SUNFLOWERS. It is commonly supposed that sunflowers turn to face the sun all day, but in fact the reverse is true.

SUPERHEROES. According to Prof. Wilton Beard of the Classics Department at Duck Hollow University, the superheroes in modern comic books and motion pictures, with their masks, exaggerated gestures, introspective monologues, conflicts with fate and destiny, and lives of inner torment, are in every respect equivalent to the heroes of Greek tragedy, except way dumber.

SWISS GUARDS. In spite of their name, the pope's famous Swiss Guards are recruited exclusively from Liechtenstein.

TAPE, INVISIBLE. In 1973, the LePage's company finally succeeded in formulating a truly invisible adhesive tape. Unfortunately, it proved impossible to sell a product that no one could see. Somewhere in East Liberty a warehouse still holds the original manufacturing run, but no one knows where. Treasure-seekers have been feeling

Only known photograph of the first batch of LePage's Invisible
Tape, which disappeared shortly after this photograph was taken.

their way around East Liberty warehouses for years looking for it.

Tchaikovsky. All other Russian names that begin with the letter Ч are transliterated with a *Ch* in English, but Tchaikovsky's name is transliterated with a *Tch*. The anomaly is due to the acrimony of Tchaikovsky's enemies in the English-speaking music press, who wished to make sure that Tchaikovsky's name would always appear last in alphabetical lists of Russian composers.

Tea. In ancient China, adulteration of tea with such flavorings as "blackcurrant" and "blueberry vanilla swirl" was punishable by death.

Tea. Tea was in use as early as the 19th century b.c., but it never really became popular until almost two thousand years later, when the emperor Li Chi had the inspired idea of adding hot water.

Tennis. The scoring system of tennis is a relic of the days when the sport was practiced by the ancient Belgae as a fertility ritual.

Termites. Much as bees communicate information by

means of a specialized dance, termites communicate by means of a primitive form of opera.

TERNARY SCHEMA. The flight of the Ternary Schema is one of the great migrations of the avian world. From their winter home in the farthest reaches of Pentarchonia to their summer breeding grounds in the Fandango is a journey of more than fifteen thousand miles for these brave and tireless adventurers. The Fandango is only about a hundred yards from Pentarchonia, but the Ternary Schema is not a very bright bird.

TEXAS. The stars in Texas skies are so big that only one of them will fit on a flag.

THYME (*Thymus*). Several related species of the genus *Thymus* have culinary uses, but the most common of them, as its specific name implies, is *T. vulgaris*, the common or garden thyme. It may be used fresh or dried, sometimes as whole sprigs and sometimes as leaves only with the stems discarded. Thyme is relatively easy to grow, and some varieties make excellent ornamental plantings as well as culinary herbs. Newtonian thyme (*T. newtonii*), for example, brings a calming sense of order to the herb garden. Care must be taken, however, in planting some of the more exotic varieties. Relativistic thyme (*T. lorentzi*) presents entirely different aspects to different observers, in extreme cases plunging a garden into confusion and chaos and causing endless arguments among one's guests. Planck thyme (*T. minimus*), the smallest variety, is so tiny that standard horticultural theory tends to break down at this level; this species should be left to expert gardeners who are prepared to cope with its unusual demands. In folk wisdom it is said that "thyme waits for no man," a property also attributed to the closely related herb thyde.

TIDES. It was long believed that tides were caused by the gravitational attraction of the moon pulling on the water. In fact tides are cause by repulsion, the waters of the ocean having an innate antipathy to any body so dry as the moon.

TIME. Chronologists were deeply embarrassed by the recent discovery that Coordinated Universal Time is more than three years slow, but it is too late to make a correction now.

According to Schroedinger, merely observing the passage of time by means of a clock or watch wastes quite a bit of the stuff.

TINSEL. Overharvesting has led to a drastic decline in the natural tinsel forests of the Amazon, leading some environmentalists to predict that tinsel will be entirely extinct by 2050.

TOMATO. Only its susceptibility to frost prevents a single tomato plant from eventually covering the North American continent.

The common argument over whether a tomato is a vegetable or a fruit is based on a fundamental misconception. A tomato is actually a sedentary animal related to the corals.

A tomato seedling planted upside-down will grow into a potato.

TRAINS. Hero of Alexandria invented the O-scale model railroad; it would be another two millennia before full-size railroads were invented.

TREES, ARTIFICIAL. Artificial trees are grown from plastic seeds in specially lighted factories.

TREES. The seed of a tree contains all the material necessary for the growth of the tree throughout its life.

Some of the smaller tree seeds are denser than neutron stars.

TRUMAN, HARRY S. Harry Truman's middle name was Salathiel, but he detested the name and prohibited its use in official documents.

TUNA. Tuna have long been the dolphins' only natural enemies, but tuna marked "dolphin safe" has been specially bred to be less aggressive.

Commercial tuna is now grown directly in the can.

TURKEY. Benjamin Franklin proposed the turkey as the national bird of the United States of America; but, after acrimonious debate in Congress, it was edged out by the plastic lawn flamingo.

TYLER, JOHN. John Tyler was annexed by the Republic of Texas in 1845.

TYPEWRITERS. The Daugherty is generally considered the first successful "visible" typewriter. Before the Daugherty, typewriters were invisible, which greatly limited their utility.

TYRANNOSAURUS REX. The well-known *Tyrannosaurus rex*

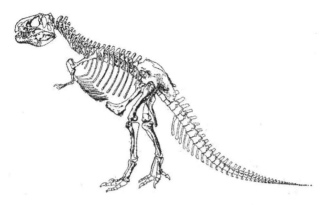

ABOVE: Type specimen of *Tyrannosaurus rex* as preserved in the
Carnegie Museum. BELOW: Speculative reconstruction.

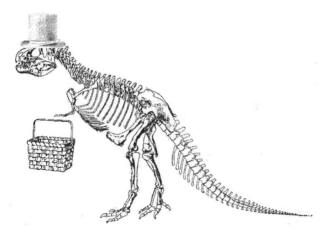

was a large and powerful dinosaur of the Cretaceous period, the last of the three ages of the Mesozoic Era or Age of Dinosaurs.

The name "*Tyrannosaurus rex*" is a Greco-Latin hybrid meaning "king tyrant lizard," but—as with most of the dinosaurs—our impressions of this creature have been considerably revised since it was named. The Tyrannosaurus was, we know now, neither a king nor a tyrant, nor for that matter a lizard. Only the ingrained taxonomical conservatism of paleontologists prevents them from coming up with a more descriptive name for it.

Modern paleontologists believe that the Tyrannosaurus spent most of its waking hours gathering wild flowers by streams of flowing water. Flowers first evolved during the Cretaceous period, and the Tyrannosaurus' bipedal posture and small forelimbs perfectly adapted it to carrying baskets of colorful blooms, which it would then present to a potential mate. These bouquets alone, however, were not enough to ensure success. The Tyrannosaurus had therefore evolved a bright and exceedingly toothy smile, with which to charm its beloved and disarm her resistance.

The diet of Tyrannosaurus consisted mostly of small heart-shaped candies with two-word slogans printed on them. It supplemented these with expensive chocolates when it could get them.

Allegorically, the Tyrannosaurus represents *unrequited love*.

UMBRELLA. The umbrella never achieved real popularity until the general public overcame the ancient superstition that it was unlucky to open one out of doors.

UMBRIA. The ancient Umbrian language was related to Latin, but only by marriage.

UNICORNS. Unicorns are found in enchanted forests and other underdeveloped places, where they use their spiral horns to drill in the ground for truffles, voles, and other flora. These they dispose of at roadside souvenir stands, which are the unicorns' chief source of income. Although the unicorn is sometimes portrayed as a rare beast in outdated literature, in recent years the population of unicorns has exploded, partly owing to the elimination in many places of rocs and other natural predators. Many suburban homeowners even in large metropolitan areas have reported unicorn damage to

Unicorn, from a late medieval German treatise on pest control.

their houses and yards. Such damage usually takes the form of perfectly round holes in gardens and walls, often accompanied by neo-fascist graffiti. The most efficacious method of repelling unicorns is to ignore them, thus depriving them of the attention on which they thrive. The unicorn is sometimes said to have inspired the myth of the narwhal, a fantastical beast said to have one horn and swim in the northern oceans; but, aside from the horn, the similarities are few, and it is safest to regard the narwhal as a creature of pure mythology.

UNITED KINGDOM. Today he is remembered mostly as the Prime Minister, but in the 1970s Gordon Brown was a very popular lounge singer in the West End.

UNITED STATES. There are actually fifty-one states in the United States of America, but most people lose track somewhere in the middle of counting them.

UNIVERSE. So-called "parallel universes" are, technically speaking, tangential rather than parallel.

The entire universe is actually upside-down, but our eyes automatically adjust to compensate.

UNIVERSITY. The first "university" was exactly the size of the entire universe (thus the name). Centuries of progress in miniaturization have produced the relatively tiny universities we know today.

URBAN DEVELOPMENT. One of the first regulations issued by the new Department of Housing and Urban Development specified that every city with a Standard Metropolitan Statistical Area over a million in population must have one suburb named Arlington.

VACUUM. It is not true that nature abhors a vacuum; nature vacuums every Tuesday, and she can't help it if people track dust all over the planet in between times.

VANILLA. Of all the common spices, Vanilla is the only one that is extracted from a corsage.

VEGETARIAN. A diet consisting mostly of meat is technically described as "vegetarian at one remove."

VENUS FLY-TRAP. The Venus Fly-Trap is a carnivorous plant that, as its name implies, can fly, soaring through the skies of the Carolinas in search of its prey. It is named for the goddess Venus on account of its excessive vanity, and indeed it will swoop down on small folding mirrors, lipsticks, and such other portable cosmetics as it may easily make off with before their owners are warned of its approach. Little is known of its habits and physiology, mostly on account of its habit of digesting professors of botany who venture too close to its lair. In its rapid movement it is similar to the Sensitive Plant (*Mimosa pudica*); the latter, however, as its Latin name implies, is ashamed of itself for undetermined reasons, and uses its capacity to move for the purpose of withdrawing itself from unwelcome attention. In the wild, the Venus Fly-Trap is currently listed as endangered, owing to invasion of its habitat by helicopters and commercial airliners. It is, however, frequently cultivated as a novelty by the adventurous and the ignorant, some of whom have survived to this day, though many are missing one or more limbs. As long as it is fed a steady diet of meter readers and security-system salesmen, the Venus Fly-Trap will grow contentedly in the home for many years.

VERNE, JULES. In *L'Île à hélice*, the noted pioneer of science fiction Jules Verne predicted the modern cardboard pizza box with astonishing accuracy.

VIA APPIA. Archaeologists excavating along the shoulder of the famous Via Appia have discovered a four-foot obelisk bearing the remains of painted decoration in alternating horizontal stripes of white and orange. So far, no one has been able to determine the purpose of the object.

VIKINGS. Medieval lore had it that the Vikings could sail into the wind—a reputation that added much to the dread and consternation of their enemies. In reality, it was a simple optical illusion, which the Vikings created by affixing a figurehead to the stern of each ship.

VIRGINIA. The Commonwealth of Virginia has never officially renounced its claim to the territories currently occupied by Tennessee, Kentucky, West Virginia, Ohio, western Pennsylvania, Indiana, Illinois, Wisconsin, Michigan, and Canada. Although no attempt has been made to enforce the claims since the early 1800s, long-time Virginia-watchers believe that Richmond is simply biding its time.

VULGAR LATIN. By today's standards, so-called "Vulgar Latin" was really quite polite.

WAGNER. For his final opera, *Parsifal*, Richard Wagner had originally written his hero's leitmotiv as a single D$\#$ played on a trombone and held for sixteen bars. His wife talked him out of it.

WASHINGTON, D.C. When the British invaded Washington in 1814, they marched up J Street, burning and destroying everything in their path so thoroughly that the street has never been rebuilt.

WASHINGTON, GEORGE. George Washington is an entirely mythical figure. The best scholarship indicates that the first truly historical President of the United States was James Monroe.

Besides his wooden teeth, George Washington is also said to have had Fiberglas toenails.

WATER. Water cannot be compressed by force, but it will respond cheerfully to a polite request.

WATERMELON. So-called "seedless" watermelons are de-seeded in sweatshops throughout the Southeast, most notably in the area around Darien, Georgia. It is notorious that most of the melon deseeders are paid less than a dollar per seed.

WAYNE, ANTHONY. The Revolutionary War general "Mad" Anthony Wayne earned his nickname at the Battle of Green Spring, when, faced with almost certain disaster against the overwhelmingly superior numbers of Cornwallis' army, he dressed as a fluffy pink bunny and sang "I'm a Little Teapot" as he hopped straight through enemy lines.

WEBSTER, NOAH. Noah Webster, the noted lexicographer, was originally Balinese; he learned the English language by reading the backs of cereal boxes.

WHITE CHRISTMAS. Irving Berlin wrote the song "White Christmas" as a throwaway commercial jingle for White's Department Store in Greensburg. He was rather embarrassed when it achieved a certain measure of popularity nationwide.

WITCH HAZEL. Witch hazel is actually one of the few herbs that are completely useless to witches.

WOLF. The wolf is a variety of dog that has traded servility for independence, and consequently abundance for mere subsistence;—from which you may draw any moral you like. Wolves live mainly on a diet of kindly old grandmothers, but many wolves suffer from a type of bulimia that renders them unable to keep their supper down. Their attempts at obtaining fresher prey, no matter how cunningly devised, invariably fail, leaving the wolves hungry and frustrated. They may in extreme cases turn to scavenging in the grocery sections of large

A Yorkshire terrier in its primitive form.

discount department stores, but their limited budgets and poor comparison-shopping skills put them at a disadvantage here as well. Some wolves are therefore lured back into domesticity; and it is suspected, though never more than whispered in dog-fancying circles, that standard poodles are simply wolves that have fallen into the hands of a hairdresser.

Wolves are also noted for their peculiar habit of adopting and nursing human infants with remarkable destinies ahead of them. How a wolf can sense which infant is a child of destiny is still imperfectly understood; but it is known that wolves possess an olfactory sense far keener than our own, and it may be that certain human children simply smell like destiny.

In spite of the animals' superficial differences, biologists regard the Grey Wolf, the Red Wolf, and the Yorkshire Terrier as varieties of the same species. Wolves can be successfully domesticated with some effort; whether the same can be said of the Yorkshire Terrier is a matter requiring further study.

Allegorically, the wolf represents independence, and specifically what a fat lot of good independence does us if we are not also independently wealthy.

WORLD, END OF. A professor at Pierre Technical College in South Dakota has calculated the exact date of the end of the world, but he refuses to reveal it until he is granted tenure.

WORLD WAR I. In the confusion at the beginning of the First World War, the Austro-Hungarian Empire accidentally declared war on Paraguay. The matter was quickly forgotten in the press of subsequent events, with the result that Paraguay is still technically at war with either Austria or Hungary (no one is certain which one).

WREATH. The Christmas wreath was originally an instrument of execution. Although the ancient Druidic custom of hanging a maiden from an evergreen tree to ensure the return of spring has died out in most of its former range, the jolly symbolism of the evergreen noose remains one of our most cherished midwinter traditions.

WRIGHT BROTHERS. Orville and Wilbur Wright are well known for their invention of the first successful powered airplane. It is less well known that Orville could also fly without the airplane, an ability of which his brother was always bitterly envious.

WRITING. Early Greek writing was often written left to

right on one line, then right to left on the next, and so on. This style of writing was known as *boustrophedon*, or "as the ox ploughs," because oxen were often given light fiction to read to ease the boredom of ploughing fields day after day.

WYOMING. Since 1994, by an act of the state legislature, Wyoming license plates have been manufactured in the shape of the state of Wyoming; but so far no one has noticed.

YACHTING. In 2003, a number of well-publicized incidents finally forced the World Yachting Commission to ban the longstanding but controversial practice of blowing really hard over and over again into the sails to gain a little extra speed.

YELLOW-GREEN. A decision of the Supreme Court (Peterson vs. Binney & Smith, 1962) determined by a 7-2 vote that "greenish yellow" and "yellow-green" are the same color.

YUGOSLAVIA. At the end of the First World War, an anonymous diplomat sketched the nation of "Yugo-slavia" on a map of the Balkans as a joke. He did not anticipate that he would be the only statesman in Europe with an ironical sense of humor, but by the time he revealed his pleasantry it was too late.

Z_EBRA_. The zebra is a mythical beast, but the myth is so pervasive and tenacious that no effort of the zoologists has succeeded in suppressing it. If you have seen a zebra at a zoo, it was really a horse painted with stripes in order to placate the thousands of visitors who demand to see a zebra.

Z_OLA_, E_MILE_. Astonishingly, it is reported that Emile Zola believed his surreal soap opera *Nana* was "realistic."

Z_UCCHINI_. In the wild, zucchini are ferociously carnivorous; but they pose no danger in the garden, as long as they are treated with suitable deference.

ADVERTISEMENT.

GET YOUR NEWS ON PAPER!

READERS! DID YOU KNOW THAT the Dispatch, Pittsburgh's most respected news source, is also available on *paper?* Unlike traditional on-line news sites, news *papers* require no power and no Internet connection, and are *guaranteed* free of trojans and malware! *Paper* is the news medium of the future! Stop by our office today and pick up a free sample.

ADVERTISEMENT.

Mrs. Sweet's Finishing School for Girls

❀❀❀❀❀❀❀

Do you have a daughter, niece, or easily abducted young female neighbor in an unfinished state? Rely on Mrs. Sweet to apply the requisite gloss to your "diamond in the rough." Our young ladies are perfect patterns of feminine accomplishment, suitable for framing or mounting. A 35% discount applies for multiple admissions, so round up every girl on your block and start making your neighborhood a better and healthier place!

Nota bene.—Mrs. Sweet has asked us to inform the general public that it is advisable not to speak the word *scherzando* to any of her alumnae, as Mrs. Sweet is reserving that word for a *special occasion.*

❀❀❀❀❀❀❀

Mrs. Sweet's Finishing School for Girls

Chartiers Avenue, McKees Rocks
Next to the Bowling Alley

10357826R00095

Made in the USA
Charleston, SC
29 November 2011